# CHEAP THRILLS

# CHEAP THRILLS

## Great Montreal Meals
## for Under $10

**1998 EDITION**

**Nancy Marrelli**
**Simon Dardick**

# Véhicule Press

Special appreciation to Vicki Marcok.
Thank you to Josh Freed for permission to
reprint "The Sex of Restaurants," from his
book, *Fear of Frying & Other Fax of Life*
(Véhicule Press).

Cover photograph: Thomas Königsthal, Jr.
Cover styling: Louise Vidricaire
Cover art direction: J.W. Stewart
Cover imaging: André Jacob
Typesetting: Simon Garamond
Printing: AGMV-Marquis Inc.

Dépôt légal, Bibliothèque nationale du Québec
and National Library of Canada,
fourth quarter 1997.

CANADIAN CATALOGUING IN PUBLICATION DATA
Main entry under title:
Cheap thrills : great Montreal
meals for under $10

1998 ed.
Includes index.
ISBN 1-55065-098-X

1. Restaurants–Quebec (Province)–Montreal–
Guidebooks. I. Marrelli, Nancy
II. Dardick, Simon, 1943-

TX907.5.C22M6 1997      647.95714'28
C97-900985-5

Véhicule Press, P.O.B. 125, Place du Parc Station,
Montreal, Quebec H2W 2M9
http://www.cam.org/~vpress
Distributed by GDS

Printed in Canada

# Contents

# This book would not have been possible without our reviewers...

Aldo Marchini
Vicki Marcok
Maria Marrelli
Nancy Marrelli
Heather MacNeill
Ludovique Matthey
Diana McNeill
Savin Mhaiki
Sharon Musgrove
Vincent Ouellette
Beatrice Pearson
Johanne Pelletier
Anna Phelan-Cox
Shelley Pomerance
Marika Pruska-Carroll
Monty Raider
Mark Rennie
Darquise Rheault
Dave Rosen
Ellen Servinis
Mark Shainblum
Caroline Sigouin
Emily Sims
Kit Szanto
George Szanto
Philip Szporer
Louis Toner
André Vanasse
Richard Weiss
Rex Williams
Don Winkler
Janice Zubalik
Chantal Zumbrunn

# Introduction

We all need cheap thrills!

Our eating out habits have changed. There was a time when we went out to dinner mostly for special occasions. These days, we eat out more frequently because of our lifestyle—we are busy, we cook only on the weekend, we are single parents, we are working—or we simply cannot face the prospect of making a meal and we need to eat out! Eating out is also a pleasurable social activity. It takes us out of our homes, away from the familiar and into unknown territory. Because we eat out more frequently we often want to do it on a budget. But, we also want it to be good. We want a cheap thrill!

The first *Cheap Thrills* was created in 1994 because we realized we were in a rut. It wasn't a bad rut, just boring. We had a few favourite and familiar neighbourhood restaurants which we would return to again and again because the food was good, the service was friendly, and the prices were reasonable. But we needed some new affordable favourites! We knew friends and colleagues also had their own good and inexpensive standbys, and so the idea for this guide was born. If we shared information, we could all expand our repertoire of good places to eat in Montreal for ten dollars or less.

We asked people we knew to tell us about their favourite low-cost restaurant. The ground rules were simple. The food had to be good, and the prices had to be around $10 or less for dinner, before taxes, tip, or wine. What a response! People were delighted to share their favourite haunts and they provided detailed facts about the restaurant—some based on many visits over the years, and sometimes new or recent discoveries. Many of the restaurants were suggested by more than one person. When the book first appeared in 1994 it was an enormous success.

This 1998 edition includes more than 50 new restaurants. We went about it the same way and the list of contributors is on page seven. In the last two years some places have disappeared or have become too expensive for this guide—those those entries have been removed. Others are gone not because they are not good but because we wanted to enlarge the selection. Some of the restaurants which remain from the first edition are what we call Cheap Thrill Classics—places which are so wonderful that they are reliable standbys and will remain so. Some of the newer or less familiar restaurants, even if they are good now, have to demonstrate that they have staying power.

As in the first edition, some restaurants are included simply because the food is good, regardless of décor or atmosphere. Others are included because they offer something special, or provide good food in settings which are suitable for a special night out. The reviews will give you a glimpse into the kind of food offered, the price range, and the atmosphere, to help you match the restaurant to your mood and requirements.

The index and the lists at the back of the book are intended to help you find somewhere to eat which will strike your fancy. The restaurants are listed in alphabetical order, but see Josh Freed's description ("The Sex of Restaurants") to see what that means!

*Cheap Thrills* contains an amazing spectrum of wonderful food places. It is truly a celebration of Montreal's amazing diversity. We are fortunate indeed to be able to share food cultures from around the world and to have access to a staggering array of different kinds of food.

Newcomers often open restaurants and cook the food which is familiar and traditional for them. This gives us all the opportunity to experience diverse cultural and culinary traditions. Many of the restaurant owners and chefs who appear in this book are anxious to share their traditions and cuisines with us. Montrealers have responded with enthusiasm to the culinary bounty which we have access to in our cosmopolitan city. For a long time we have loved pasta and pizza; we embraced souvlaki, couscous, mussels, dumplings, pesto, sushi, curries, and countless other foods. We are learning to love injera, pupusas, roti, tamales, and shawarma, and who knows what else! We increase our dining pleasure and, more importantly, enlarge our world when people share their best cooking traditions with us.

Nancy Marrelli
Simon Dardick

## What is a Cheap Thrill?

The restaurants in this book generally offer meals at dinner for $10 or less. This does not mean that every meal in the restaurant will be $10 or less, but there should be a reasonable selection in that price range, at dinner, and before taxes, tip, and wine. Most prices are indicated.

Restaurants change constantly. Menus, owners, and restaurants are in constant flux. The information in this book was current at the time of publication, but be advised that things change rapidly and without notice. It's a good idea to call first.

## How to Find a Montreal Restaurant

Restaurants in Quebec can be listed in the phone book many different ways. One never knows if the name of a particular restaurant begins with 'Café,' 'Bistro,' or 'Restaurant.' The chances are you will never find it. It may be listed as 'Le' or 'La'—even the gender of the restaurant becomes important! To simplify your life, the alphabetical list that follows lists all the restaurants in this book under several variations so that you will be sure to find what you are looking for. For example, Café Presto is listed under 'Café' and 'Presto,' and Restaurant Sénégalaise can be found under 'Restaurant' and 'Sénégalaise.' Josh Freed's humorous and instructive essay on the gender of restaurants is a 'must-read' on the subject. As a public service we are pleased to include it at the back of the book. (*See* "The Sex of Restaurants.")

# ALPHABETICAL LIST OF RESTAURANTS

## A
Agostini
Amelio's
Anecdote (L')
Apna Tandoor
Au Messob d'Or

## B
Bangkok
Baroque (Bistro)
Bedouin's House
Belle Maison
Binerie Mont-Royal (La)
Bistro Baroque
Bistro Le Porto
Bistro Le Relais des Sultans
Bistro Unique (Le)
Briskets
Byblos

## C
Café Les Entretiens
Café International
Café Presto
Café Santropol
Caribbean Curry House
Carreta (La)
Chalet Bar B-Q
Champs
Chez Doval
Chez Gatsé
Chez Soi
Chez Tung
Copoli

Cosmo Famous Snack Bar
Cristal de Saigon

## D
Dong Que
Doval (Chez)

## E
Elio Pizzeria
Encore Une Fois
Entretiens (Café les)
Ernie & Ellie's Place
Farrouj

## G
Galaxie Diner
Gatsé
Genuine Restaurant
Grano

## H
Harmonie d'Asie (L')

## I
International (Café)
Iza

## J
Jardin du Cari
Java U
Just Noodles

## L
Los Planes

## M
Ma-am-m Bolduc!
Manzo Pizza
Mazurka

McKibbin's Pub
Mediterranéen (Le)
Messob d'Or (Au)
Metropole (La)
Montreal Hebrew Delicatessen
Moules & Cie
Motta (Pizza)
Mr. Steer

## O
Okambo

## P
Paryse (La)
Pattaya
Peel Pub
Peter's Cape Cod
Petit Alep (Le)
Petite Marche (La)
Philippine Village
Pho Bac
Pho Hoa
Pick's
Pin Restaurant (Le)
Pizza Motta
Planes (Los)
Porto (Bistro le)
Portugualia (Rotisserie)
Presto (Café)
Pushap

## R
Relais des Sultans (Bistro le)
Restaurant Sénégalaise
Restaurant Steve-Anna
Rosie's
Rotisserie Portugalia

## S

Sabouyouma
St-Viateur Bagel & Café
Sans Menu
Santropol (Café)
Schwartz's
Sénégalaise (Restaurant)
Soi (Chez)
Souvenirs de Bangkok
Steve-Anna (Restaurant)
Sun Shing

## T

Tasca
Tehran
Toasteur (Le)
Tramontane (La)
Tung (Chez)
Tutto Bene

## U

Unique (Le Bistro)

## V

Villa Wellington
Village Mon Nan

# AGOSTINI

**5545 Upper Lachine Road** (near Girouard,
Vendôme métro, 90 or 104 bus)
485-0235
Hours: 8 a.m.-10 p.m. Monday-Saturday, closed Sunday
Credit cards: none
Licence: yes
Wheelchair access: yes

Agostini is a family restaurant in NDG with fabulous
Italian food.

This is home cooking at its best. Breakfast includes
Italian sausages if you wish ($1.99-$2.99). Three specials
($6-$8) are available all day and include homemade soup
or salad, main course, dessert, and beverage. Choices (usually meat, pasta, and fish) can include veal parmesan,
tortellini Val D'Aousta (cream/almonds/chives), pennini
arrabiata, luscious manicotti, baked fish. The à la carte
menu includes veal (parmesan or marsala $8), lasagna
($6.50), gnocchi ($6.50), and pizza choices (8"-l6", $4.75-
$17). But when you crave an Italian sausage submarine
this is the place! They are made to order on a crusty bun,
with a browned split sausage, fried onions cooked to
melting perfection, tomato, coleslaw or lettuce, optional
hot sauce—a messy delight, good to the last crumb! Pig
out with the 14" ($6.50) if you must but the 7" ($3.75) is
usually enough. Fresh fruit is the best dessert bet. Espresso
($1.25) and cappuccino ($1.50) are excellent.

The restaurant is pleasant and bright (with tablecloths),
but not plush. Children are welcome, and service is friendly
and efficient, although hectic at lunch. Maria and Ezio
Agostini arrived from Italy in the late 1950s and they run
the restaurant with their children Mario and Antoinietta.
Parking is not a problem, and take out and free delivery
are available. Prices even include taxes. This is a real
find—food just like your Italian mama made—if you were
lucky enough to have one!

# AMELIO'S

**201 Milton** (near Ste-Famille, 24, 55 80 or 144 bus)
845-8396
Hours: Tuesday-Friday 11:30 a.m.-9:30 p.m., Saturday &
Sunday 4-9 p.m., closed Monday
Credit cards: none
BYOB
Wheelchair access: no

Amelio's is a favourite neighourhood restaurant,
specializing in good pasta and pizza for small budgets in
the student-dominated area between McGill and Boulevard
St-Laurent.

Main dishes include fresh daily pasta and pizza, and a
variety of submarines ($3.85). Pasta sauces are homemade
and choices include tomato, meat, vegetarian, green or rosé
sauce ($5-$6.50). Ravioli, tortellini, ($6-$7) and lasagna
($6.75) are also available. Meatballs ($2) and extra sauce
($1.50-$2.25) are optional. The lasagna with green noodles
and meat sauce is especially delicious ($6.75). The pizzas
are very good with small ($5.50-$7.25), medium ($8.10-
$10.75), and large ($13.10-$17.25) sizes available in a num-
ber of different combinations, including five cheeses.
Whole wheat dough is available for small pizzas, and extra
pizza toppings are $1 each. Portions are generous and food
is dependably fresh, tasty, and well prepared. Salads are
available as is garlic bread ($1.35). Desserts include apple
pie ($2), tiramisu ($3), and cheesecake with raspberry
sauce ($3.50).

The atmosphere is warm and friendly and the crowd is
usually young and somewhat noisy. The large square room
is comfortable and pleasant, with about 20 tables and
seating for about 50 people. Service is friendly and
efficient. George and Chris Scodras are the owners and
they have been in business for 25 years. Amelio's offers
excellent value and a friendly atmosphere.

# L'ANECDOTE

**801 Rachel East** (near St-Hubert, métro Mont-Royal,
or 29 bus)
526-7967
Hours: Monday-Friday 7:30 a.m.-10 p.m., Saturday-Sunday
9 a.m.- 10 p.m.
Credit cards: Interac
Licenced: yes
Wheelchair access: no

L'Anecdote could be described as an upscale neighbourhood diner on the Plateau Mont-Royal.

The menu includes a full range of breakfasts at reasonable prices and a great selection of salads ($4.50-$7.95),
and omelets ($3.95/plain, $7.95/smoked salmon). Sandwiches are wide ranging and reasonably priced: grilled
cheese ($2.95), and a croque-monsieur ($7.25 with chips).
L'Anecdote absolutely shines when it comes to burgers.
Le petit anecdote ($4.45) includes emmenthal cheese,
mushrooms, bacon, tomato, lettuce, and mayonnaise—
other combos are also available. The menu includes tofu
hot dogs ($1.75), generous club sandwiches ($7.75), and
steak frites ($9.95). The fries are homemade and excellent.
Desserts include cheesecake, cake, and pie—good and
generous portions. Espresso and cappuccino are available
at reasonable prices. For kids under ten there are special
meals. The menu is quite extensive and there is something
for everyone.

L'Anecdote has a 1950s/1960s feel to it, and it is as
comfortable and relaxed as an old pair of jeans. The back
section is the result of an expansion a few years ago, while
the front is the original restaurant. Service is efficient.

# APNA TANDOOR

**1001 Jean Talon West** (near Birnam, métro l'Acadie,
92, 16 bus)
277-1661
Hours: Sunday-Thursday 11 a.m.-11 p.m., Friday, Saturday
11 a.m.-1 p.m.
Credit cards: no
Licence: yes
Wheelchair access: no

This is an informal Indian neighbourhood restaurant which serves a variety of terrific food at very reasonable prices.

There are no specials but the menu includes a wide range of possibilities—most dishes are $3-$8, and meals will average $4-$10. The thalis are excellent combinations of meat, vegetables, nan, and salad ($3.95-$5.95). The nan is very good, prepared to order in the tandoor oven (whose charcoal incidentally gently scents the whole place). The generous tandoor chicken ($7) is superb. North Indian standards like biryanis, curries, and chicken tikka are well prepared and very reasonably priced. The Indian sweets are inexpensive and many are excellent. The best deal is a take-out bag of orange coloured bits of sweet jalebi (about $1 for a half pound).

Four Punjabi men, who speak little English or French, run the restaurant which is comfortable but nondescript. By far the best decoration is the inviting stacks of Indian pastries at the front, available by the pound for take-out. Washroom facilities are downstairs and through the truck school next door. The South Asian surroundings are part of the atmosphere, including the Indian video store on Jean Talon just to the east where sweets are made in the back of the store! All this amid the noisy traffic of Jean Talon?

# BANGKOK

**1616 Ste-Catherine West** (in Le Faubourg, 3rd floor,
métro Guy, 15 bus)
Hours: 10 a.m.-9 p.m.
Credit cards: none
Licence: no
Wheelchair access: yes

Yes, you can find really fine Thai food at affordable prices
in a downtown food mall!

The Bangkok, in Le Faubourg, has exceptionally good
Thai food. The chicken soup ($2 plus 25¢ with coconut
milk) is outstanding, made to order every time, with chunks
of fresh chicken and lemon grass. The taste is pure, and
clear—arguably the best chicken soup in the city. Set
specials ($5.50) are a good bet, and include soup or two
spring rolls, with chicken or beef curry, ginger beef, or
chicken with cashews. The large à la carte menu includes
the sublime eggplant Bangkok (with chicken) ($4.95),
excellent garlic pepper shrimp ($6.95), and the traditional
pad Thai ($4.50 with chicken), which is superb. BBQ duck
with coconut milk ($5.50) is outstanding. Vegetarian
choices are extensive, spring rolls are homemade, and no
pork is served. The only problem is to choose!

Don't be put off by the location. All dishes except the
specials are cooked to order, and the food has all the
complex flavours and textures of Thai food. Any item on
this menu is recommended without hesitation. The chef
owner is Somphop Vichenker, and can she cook! She
creates magic in plain view in this food mall stand. She
rarely leaves her spot at the burners, and everything meets
her demanding standards. Husband Santisuk and daughter
Patty handle the front with grace and courtesy. Don't miss
Bangkok, it's too good to be true!

# BEDOUIN'S HOUSE/LA MAISON DU BEDOUIN

**1616 Ste-Catherine West** (in Le Faubourg, 3rd floor, métro Guy, 15 bus)
Hours: 11 a.m.-9 p.m.
935-0236
Credit cards: none
Licence: no
Wheelchair access: yes

The Bedouin's House offers wonderful North African food in the most unlikely of places, le Faubourg.

The Bedouin's House is the new incarnation of Casablanca which used to be in the space adjacent to it. The menu is limited but everything is delectable. The specials ($4.25 or $4.99 for a combo plate) are a series of tagines (Moroccan stew)—sausages, Moroccan meatballs, saffron chicken , vegetables, and beef. Each has its own rich, tasty gravy and comes with rice and two salads. A meatball or merguez sandwich is only $2.99, including salad. Pastilla (chicken with almonds and a delicate hint of rose water $4.75) is a delight. Hearty harira chickpea soup ($1.75) is delicious. Everything is made on the premises using halal meat. The mint tea, made with fresh mint, comes with sugar unless you request otherwise, and is served in metal pots with tiny glass cups. Moroccan pastries are $1.10 and freshly made donuts ($.95) are usually available by late afternoon.

Khalil and Hamid (both from Morocco) took over the old Casablanca and moved it into a bigger space in the fall of 1997 and the quality of the food remains excellent. This is a great place for lunch when the Faubourg is busy, but also quite pleasant in the evening when it is quieter and more dimly lit. It's hard to believe that you can get such wonderful food from a fast food stand!

# BELLE MAISON

**3967 St-Antoine West** (near du Couvent, métro St-Henri/
Lionel Groulx, 78 bus)
933-7421
Hours: Monday-Friday, noon-2 p.m., 5:30-9 p.m., closed
Saturday and Sunday
Credit cards: none
Licence: Beer & wine
Wheelchair access: one step at street level

This is a busy but friendly restaurant with a wide selection
of Szechuan and Malaysian food.

The menu includes both hot and spicy and more tame
selections. House specialties include dumplings ($4), broccoli
shrimp ($7), ginger chicken ($6). The cashew chicken ($6,
not spicy) is a particularly good bet as is szechuan chicken
($6). There is a dinner special which includes hot and sour
soup, imperial rolls, and rice for $5. Most dishes are $6.50-
$7.50, shrimp dishes are $7.50-$8.50. The combos are
tasty and offer good value with a menu for two at $16.50
and a menu for five (which includes nine dishes) at $57.95.
Both Chinese and micro brewery beers are available.

This family-run restaurant has an open kitchen and all
the delightful cooking smells waft through the large street-
level room to whet the appetite. The husband cooks, the
wife deals with customers, and various relatives wait on
tables. Decoration is basic but cheerful with Chinese decorations and posters on the walls. This is a very busy place
and you may have to wait, but the service is pleasant and
friendly. Kids are welcome but make sure they are not
starving! This restaurant is in a pleasant residential section
of St-Henri. It's on a busy street but the green space of
Parc Saint-Henri and some interesting Montréal
architecture are all close by. Street parking is limited to
one hour only before 6 p.m. and unlimited after 6.

# LA BINERIE MONT-ROYAL

**367 Mont-Royal East** (St-Denis, métro Mont-Royal)
285-9078
Hours: Monday-Friday 6 a.m.-10 p.m., Saturday 6 a.m.-4 p.m., Sunday 8 a.m.-3 p.m.
Credit cards: none
Licence: no
Wheelchair access: no

La Binerie is in a time warp: it's a 1940s working class diner on Plateau Mont-Royal.

The day starts with breakfast ($2.10-$4.65) for various combinations of eggs, bacon, sausage, toast, cretons, and baked beans. The special is $3.90 for baked beans and bread, $5.35 with sausages. The complete three-course lunch or dinner includes pea soup, dessert, and beverage. It costs between $5.69 and $6.75 and you choose from items like macaroni with meat, beef with cabbage, shepherd's pie, tourtière, ragoût de boulettes, sausages, cretons, etc. The "Assiette Maison" ($8.24) combines the tourtière, the ragoût de boulettes, and baked beans—all the house specialties—and this is the most expensive item on the menu. Dessert is the Binerie's famous pudding chômeur. The food is all made here, with closely guarded recipes, and the food is stick-to-your ribs and substantial. It's hard to leave here hungry!

This is a small friendly place, a family-run business with only 11 stools at the counter and four tables, and the service is prompt and friendly, but not intrusive. Everything is basic and there are absolutely no frills. Started in 1940, this business has stayed in the family and everything is very much like it always has been. La Binerie serves the kind of food that makes you feel like you should go out and chop down some trees! La Binerie is all about good, simple, wholesome food, at low, low prices.

# BISTRO BAROQUE

**190 Ste-Catherine West** (in Complexe Desjardins/Jeanne-Mance, métro Place-des-Arts)
844-3912
Hours: Monday-Friday 6 a.m.-midnight, Saturday-Sunday
 8 a.m.-midnight
Credit cards: Visa, MC, Amex, Interac
Licence: yes
Wheelchair access: yes

Bistro Baroque serves quality breakfast, lunch, and dinner in a pleasant setting, right in Complexe Desjardins.

Breakfast starts early here and includes eggs, omelets, pancakes and freshly squeezed juices ($2.75, $3.95). Daily specials are available at lunch or dinner ($7.95-$12.95) and come with a main course (pasta, quiche, etc.), salad and beverage. The pasta choices come with a generous salad, and choice of sauce ($8.55-$10.95). Vegetarian lasagna ($9.55) is creamy and beautifully sauced and comes with a large salad. Salads are excellent and very generous, and include avocado/shrimp ($8.95), spinach/orange ($7.55), and Waldorf ($7.25). Sandwiches are generous, served on baguette, country loaf, or pita. Choices include prosciutto ($8.55) or Black Forest ham with cheese ($7.95), all are served with a large helping of your choice of salad. The chicken pita sandwich ($8.95) is especially good with generous slices of juicy grilled chicken breast and salad.

This is a great place for dinner on your way to or from Place-des-Arts, the Spectrum, TNM, the Musée d'art contemporain, or downtown shopping. Owners Pierre and Francine opened this place in 1996 and it has become very popular. Manager André Raynald runs a tight ship, providing quality food and service in this high volume resto. In good weather the glass doors open to a terrace with outdoor seating. In winter there are theme night Wednesdays with live music.

# ᴊTRO LE PORTO

**1365 Ontario East** (near Panet, métro Beaudry, 125 bus)
527-7067
Hours: Monday-Wednesday 11 a.m.-11p.m., Thursday-Friday 11 a.m.-1 p.m., Saturday 5 p.m.-1 p.m. (closed Sunday), kitchen closes at 10 p.m. every night, but port and cheeses continue to be available
Credit cards: Visa, MC, Interac
Licence: yes
Wheelchair access: yes

This charming Portuguese bistro near the Beaudry métro serves good food and a vast selection of fine ports—both at reasonable prices!

The daily special comes with appetizer (the soups are great) and beverage. The choice always includes a pasta dish, ($6.95), a large plate of mussels ($9.95), the house specialty (grilled sardines and squid $10.95), and a meat selection. Share a generous basket of delicious croustilles maison (potato skins $2.65). Light meal selections include: Caesar salad ($5.95), burgers ($6.25-$6.95) quiche of the day ($7.25), and there is a good steak/frites napped with pepper sauce ($7.95). Fries and salad are terrific and plentiful. Desserts are very good, including a perfectly cooked crème caramel ($2.50). Porto, of course, has port—about 50 selections at any one time—and prices are very reasonable (a glass of Ferreira '91 Vintage port is $9.95). Take advantage of the good food prices to indulge in the port. The list is on a large blackboard and includes ruby, tawny, late vintage, and vintage ports. Cheese plates are available—including stilton of course. If you don't already love port, you will!

Portuguese-born Teresa Barroso was a designer and her brother Sylvestre worked in the restaurant business before they bought the two-year-old Porto in September 1997, and their attentive presence is a plus. The ambiance is good, with well-chosen Portuguese music, tablecloths, and comfortable chairs. Go to Porto for a special evening or for a simple meal with a glass or two of port and cheese.

# LE BISTRO UNIQUE

**1039 Beaubien East** (near Christophe-Colomb, métro Beaubien, 18 bus)

279-4433

Hours: Monday-Thursday 11 a.m.-10 p.m., Friday-Sunday 11 a.m.-11:30 p.m. (They close earlier if they are not busy).

Credit cards: Visa, AMEX, MC, Interac

Licence: beer and wine

Wheelchair access: yes

This is a very pleasant bistro on Beaubien with superb stuffed pastas and lots of atmosphere.

Each week there is a plat du jour available ($6-$12) which can range from mussels ($7.95) to a special salad ($5.95) or something a little more extravagant. The mussels provençale or marinara ($7.95) are flavoured nicely and are worthwhile. Pastas ($7.95-$11) are excellent, and stuffed pastas ($8.95-$13.25) are the specialty of the house. The saccatti has a well-deserved reputation— two packets of homemade pasta with an extraordinarily fine stuffing made with pine nuts, raisins, prosciutto and spinach, and decoratively pinched at the ends. The whole thing is then dressed with a luscious creamy cheese sauce. The penne arrabbiata ($8.95) is especially good. All the pasta is cooked perfectly *al dente* here and sauces are well prepared. Oysters are available in season. Excellent veal dishes are a good bet ($13.95-$14.95) if you wish to spend a little more. Pizza is and vegetarian dishes are also available. The restaurant does no deep frying so french fries are not available.

This is a nice place to spend an evening, with comfortable chairs, and low-key background music. There are rotating art exhibits on the walls and they are frequently good, adding a nice touch to an already agreeable space. When the restaurant is busy an extra room is available, and one becomes a smoking area and the other a non-smoking area. There is a pleasant outdoor terrace available in good weather. The serving staff are extremely helpful and charming.

# BRISKETS

**2055 Bishop** (at de Maisonneuve, métro Guy/Concordia, 15 or 24 bus)
843-3651, 843-3650
1073 Beaver Hall
878-3641
(Kiosks at Olympic Stadium and Eaton Centre offer a basic menu only.)

Hours: <u>Bishop</u>: Monday-Wednesday 11a.m.-10 p.m., Thursday-Saturday 11 a.m.-11 p.m., closed Sunday, except for reserved large groups
<u>Beaver Hall</u>: Monday-Friday 11 a.m.-8 p.m., closed weekends
Licence: beer and wine
Credit cards: Visa, MC, Amex
Wheelchair access: no

Briskets and smoked meat are virtually synonymous, but don't ignore the wonderful "fixings" here. They have the best onion rings in town ($3.95 for a full order, $2.95 for a half order)—crisp and freshly made, served with dill and sour cream sauce. The homemade mushrooms ($4.50/ $3.50) are crisp outside and juicy inside, and the homemade fries ($1.50) are perfectly cooked in vegetable oil. Dill pickles ($1.25) and sweet pimentos ($1.25) are also available. The smoked meat is succulent—real Montreal-style smoked meat and you can order lean, medium lean or medium. The sandwiches ($3.75) are generous portions on good rye bread. Other items on the full menu include spaghetti, hamburgers, club sandwiches, and Bavarian sausages, and there is a $4.95 luncheon special weekdays, but nobody much bothers with them.

Here smoked meat is king! Old fashioned soda fountain soft drinks ($1.50) are available in 12 flavours, including cherry coke, strawberry, and vanilla, as are ice cream floats ($2.50) and milk shakes ($3.25). You can order beer by the glass or pitcher ($2.25/$9.95).

The atmosphere is relaxed and the service is friendly.

## BYBLOS

**1499 Laurier East** (near Fabre, Laurier métro, 27 bus)
523-9396
Hours: 9 a.m.-11 p.m., closed Monday
Credit cards: Visa, MC, Amex, Interac
Licence: yes
Wheelchair access: yes

This is a wonderful restaurant specializing in homestyle Persian (Iranian) food.

The appetizers are a delight here and can be combined to make an unusual meal, from such tasties as garlic chives purée ($3.25), olives with walnuts and pomegranate seeds ($4.10), cream of lentil soup flavoured with cardamom ($2.60), eggplant stuffed with a garlic yogurt mixture ($4). There are daily specials (lunch $6.95, dinner $7.35) of lamb, chicken, and fish or beef. Main course meat, vegetable or cheese turnovers ($4-$4.30) are a house specialty, as are vegetable purées ($4-$5.30). Vegetarian possibilities are interesting. On Sunday evening Le Dizzy, the national Iranian dish of lamb, lentils, potatoes, and tomatoes ($9) served in the traditional style (accompanied by herbs) is available between 5 p.m. and 10. A vegetarian version replaces lamb with eggplant. Perfumed Iranian tea accompanies both. Desserts are interesting combinations, often including such delicacies as rose water.

Byblos started out as a small cozy café. It has expanded but has kept the feel of a Mediterranean country kitchen. In summer the front window opens to create a semi-terrace. Seats are comfortable and the atmosphere is homey and friendly. There is a bar, as well as tables and booths. The restaurant is owned by Hemela Pourafzal and she is assisted by a rotating roster of relatives. Eating at Byblos is an adventure in subtle, unusual, and pleasing tastes, in a home-like environment where customers feel free to linger.

# CAFÉ LES ENTRETIENS

**1577 Laurier East** (near Fabre, métro Laurier)
521-2934
Hours: 9 a.m.- midnight
Credit cards: Visa, MC, Interac
Licence: yes
Wheelchair access: no

This Laurier East health food-style café makes you feel good.

The menu offers fresh uncomplicated food from breakfast through dinner. Breakfasts are special—a good way to start the day on a relaxed Sunday. The #4 breakfast is recommended—a choice of juice, two brown eggs, two croissants, and a cup or a bowl of café au lait, or café allongé, or hot chocolate ($6.55 with cup/$7.40 with bowl).

Appetizers include cheeses, vegetarian paté ($3.75), smoked salmon ($4.50) and pizza on azim bread ($5.50). Salads ($6.50-$7.25) are beautifully presented with a choice of vinaigrettes. Sandwiches are prepared on good tasty whole wheat bread and there is quite a selection, including cheddar cucumber ($4), brie and sprouts ($4), and egg and green pepper ($3.75). There is an interesting selection of seven 'gratins', the house specialty—slices of bread with a choice of emmenthal or cheddar cheese and many different toppings such as tuna/onion/mushroom ($5.75), hummous/onion/olive/peppers ($5.75), and ham/tomato/onion ($5.75). They are piping hot and meltingly delicious! The main plate special changes daily and is $6.95. There is an excellent selection of very good juices and fruit shakes.

This cozy place invites special confidences between friends. It's also a perfect spot to read or relax. A terrace is available in good weather. The food is so fresh and so appetizingly-garnished with market-fresh vegetables that you feel virtuous just looking at it—and it tastes good too! The service is prompt and discreet.

# CAFÉ INTERNATIONAL

**6714 St-Laurent Blvd.** (near St-Zotique, 55 bus)
495-0067
Hours: Sunday-Thursday 7 a.m.-1 a.m., Friday 7 a.m.-3 a.m.,
Saturday 8 a.m.-3 a.m.
Credit cards: Visa, MC, Interac
Licence: yes
Wheelchair access: yes

This is an authentic café in Little Italy, which serves good food and excellent coffee, and boy does it have attitude!

The menu is limited, mostly pizza and pasta ($4.50+). The cannelloni ($6.95) is especially good. The sausage sandwich ($7.25 with salad) is superb, made to order with grilled fresh Italian sausage and fried onions, on a crusty roll—one of the best in the city. The tuna salad consists of a large plate of fresh lettuce dressed with olive oil vinaigrette, and a generous portion of Italian tuna ($6.95). You can dress the tuna yourself with the selection of virgin olive oils and balsamic vinegars which are available on the bar. Simple but luxurious! There is an excellent selection of Italian pastries and biscotti. Then there is the coffee—espresso ($1.35) and cappuccino ($2.25) are the real specialty of the house. The coffees are freshly ground and expertly brewed.

There is a long counter (no stools, people stand), and simple café tables and chairs. The front windows are actually sliding doors which open out in good weather. A big TV screen quietly documents the passing international sports scene for those who are interested. As for the attitude, what a progression. The day starts with people drinking coffee and reading their papers. Later, people rendezvous with friends and sometimes lovers, while families look on in wonderment. By late evening the scene throbs with those wanting to see and be seen!

# CAFÉ PRESTO

**1244 Stanley** (near Ste-Catherine, métro Peel, 15 bus)
879-5877
Hours: 11:30 a.m.-3 p.m., 4:30 p.m.-19:30 p.m.
Credit cards: none
Licence: wine & beer
Wheelchair access: no

Café Presto is a cozy little Italian bistro in the heart of downtown where the prices are unbeatable.

The wall menu changes daily but entrée prices are always $3.95 each. The menu is mostly pasta, and the five to six choices often include penne arrabbiata, linguine paradiso (creamy rosé sauce), and spicy Italian sausage with pasta and tomato sauce. Presto salad with house dressing ($3.75) adds a nice touch, and is fresh, excellent, and varied, while the more modest green salad is $1.75. Homemade vegetable soup ($2.25) rivals your grandmother's! The food is homestyle, but obviously prepared with care and attention, which unfailingly pleases.

Café Presto is owned by Luciano and Rino Massironi. Rino is the chef and both serve out front. This is a tiny little place but there is a warm, intimate atmosphere, and less than a dozen tables. There are blue and white checked tablecloths and decorations include pictures of Marilyn Monroe and James Dean, which somehow all comes together in a space which feels comfortable and inviting, a good setting for the very good food. Rino or Luciano calculates your tab at the counter, and ceremoniously rings a cow bell once you pay! This is a little treasure—hard to find in downtown Montreal.

# CAFÉ SANTROPOL

**3990 St-Urbain** (near Duluth, métro St-Laurent, 55, 144 bus)
842-3110
Hours: Monday-Thursday 11:30 a.m.-midnight, Saturday-Sunday noon.-1 a.m., Sunday noon-midnight
Credit cards: Interac
Licence: BYOB
Wheelchair access: no

Café Santropol is a small funky oasis on the edge of the Plateau, near Jeanne-Mance park and the Main.

The food is not elaborate, but reliably good with many dairy and vegetarian dishes. The salads are fresh and interesting ($5.25, $6.25, +$1.50 to add cheese/ tofu/ham/ tuna or chicken). There is a wide assortment of interesting sandwiches ($6-$7.50) served on homemade bread, including: Killer Tomato (sun-dried tomatoes, basil, cream or cottage cheese), Santropol (roast beef, blue cheese, cream cheese), Duluth Avenue (brie, blue cheese, nuts, spices). Three-decker sandwiches are as interesting and even bigger ($7.75-$8.25). Vegetarian pies (millet, spinach/feta, $6.75) are good. The homemade soup ($2.75) is invariably delicious, and is almost a meal in itself when served with homemade bread. There are lots of teas and tisanes, and desserts ($4) are very good.

Garth, Jennifer and Jim have been working together running Santropol for more than 20 years. The space was slated to become a parking lot but after considerable protest, the adjacent houses became a co-op and the restaurant has stayed. It has a wonderful garden and terrace in good weather and feels like an oasis of calm any time of the year. Decoration is definitely funky, and there is a combination of chairs and tables, booths, and stools. Staff are friendly and helpful. One percent of the proceeds goes to various agencies that deal with hunger. Santropol is a feel-good place where you can eat well too.

# CARIBBEAN CURRY HOUSE

**6892 Victoria Avenue** (near Jean-Talon, métro Vendôme, 124 bus)
733-0828
Hours: Monday-Saturday 11 a.m.-10:00 p.m., Sunday noon-10 p.m., open "late" Friday
Credit cards: none
Licence: yes
Wheelchair access: no

Caribbean Curry House serves wonderful Indian/Trinidadian specialties in this Victoria Avenue restaurant and take-out spot.

The menu is fixed and there are no daily specials. Prices include all taxes. You can choose from among four fish dishes ($4.75-$6.95), the most popular of which is the kingfish, served with rice, plantain and/or banana, salad, and gravy. The curries are flavourful and hearty—beef ($5.95), chicken ($5.95), goat ($5.95), vegetarian ($5.25)—served with rice, potatoes, salad, and plantain and/or banana. The oxtail stew ($6.15), rich and tasty, with just the right touch of spices, is a winner, served with rice and beans. There is a selection of 13 different kinds of roti (a large flat pancake which is chock full of various fillings and is folded into a square, $3.30-$4.45 each), and they are wonderful. The nicely spiced fillings are diverse and packed with flavour! They have Jamaican beers and Caribbean rums.

Emrith Kalliecharan, an Indian Trinidadian, owns Caribbean Curry House, and has been in business since 1981. This is an informal place with lots of people of all ages coming and going. Much of the business is take-out, but there are plenty of comfortable tables and chairs for those who wish to eat in. The space is relaxed and informal, with an aquarium, decent lighting, and a very pleasant level of reggae and steel drum music. There's live music on Friday evenings. This is a good place for your very own budget island getaway!

# LA CARRETA

**350 St-Zotique East** (near Drolet, métro Beaubien or
 Jean-Talon)
278-5779
Hours: Monday-Wednesday 11:30 a.m.-11 p.m.,
Thursday-Sunday 11:30 a.m.-11 p.m.
Credit cards: none
Licence: yes
Wheelchair access: entrance OK but not washrooms

La Carreta is a neighbourhood restaurant which serves
authentic Salvadoran food.

Homemade soups are substantial and satisfying. There
is a good variety of side orders which can be combined to
make a meal ($2.25-$4), including tamales ($2.25),
burritos ($3.10), tacos, ($3), and fajitas ($2.50). These are
all very tasty and off the beaten fast food track. The
specialty of the house, however, are pupusas ($1.60-$2
ea.)—corn tortillas stuffed with a variety of fillings, and
served with a crock of spicy, marinated cabbage. They're
great, especially with the cabbage which is served liberally
by those in the know! Why has it taken Montrealers so
long to discover Salvadoran food? Fish soup ($3.85) is
also good. The food here is hearty and well prepared using
fresh ingredients—plenty of variety without being
overwhelmed by a huge menu.

This is a neighbourhood restaurant (and a favourite with
Salvadorans) where kids are welcome. Jesse and Anna
Escobar opened in 1991 and it operates as a family
business. This is a popular spot for the neighbourhood
and for Salvadorans from all over the city. Service is
friendly, efficient, and relaxed. Latin music plays in the background (except on Saturday night 7-10 when there is live
music), and the décor is homey and cluttered.

# CHALET BAR B-Q

**5456 Sherbrooke West** (métro Vendôme, 105 bus)
489-7235
Hours: Sunday-Thursday 11 a.m.-midnight,
Friday-Saturday 11 a.m.-1 a.m.
Credit cards: Visa, MC, Interac
Licence: wine and beer
Wheelchair access: Sherbrooke entrance OK, but not washrooms

Chalet Bar B-Q is a Montreal tradition which is still going strong in NDG.

Before we got cookie cutter BBQ chicken fast food outlets, and a BBQ in every back yard, there was Chalet Bar B-Q. They have been cheerfully and efficiently welcoming customers since 1944! And the chicken and BBQ sauce is still outstanding. They have a lunch special of a quarter chicken (leg $4.95/breast $5.95) with coleslaw, fries, sauce, and a beverage. After 2 p.m. a quarter chicken, fries, and BBQ sauce costs $5.50 for a leg, and $6.50 for a breast portion. A half chicken with fries is $7.70. Salad ($1.85) or coleslaw ($1.40) is extra. They also have hot chicken sandwiches ($5.25/$6.25) and have recently introduced chicken wings. But the big favourite is still beautiful rotisserie chicken, and fries cooked in vegetable oil with a fabulous BBQ sauce for dunking. Mmm mmm good!

Chalet Bar B-Q has knotty pine wood paneling throughout—the cliché Swiss chalet. There's always a good feeling about the place, and single diners, couples, and family groups all feel welcome. Most of the staff have been there a long time (one waitress since 1952), and service is prompt, friendly, and efficient, even when they are busy. The place runs like a well-oiled machine. They do a booming take-out business and deliver without charge. They have reception rooms and free parking in the rear. There are many imitators but Chalet Bar B-Q is the real thing!

# CHAMPS

**3956 St-Laurent Blvd.** (near Duluth, métro St-Laurent, 55 bus)
987-6444
Hours: 11 a.m.-3 a.m.
Credit cards: Visa, MC, Amex
Licence: yes
Wheelchair access: no

Champs is Montreal's premier sports bar. It is rated as America's third-best sports bar (after Wayne Gretsky's and Michael Jordan's).

People go to Champs to see the sports events with other fans. The food is basic—nothing fancy. The best bets are the burgers ($5.50-$6) or the wings ($5.50/10 pieces). The burgers are grilled real meat, without filler, and the wings are crispy. Rib steak ($9.95) and club sandwiches ($7) are very popular. Nachos are $5.50. They serve breakfast, in case the game you are there to see is early in the day! An assortment of draft beer is on tap ($7.50-$13 a pitcher): Black Label, St-Ambroise, Boréale, Belle Gueule, Tartan, Corona, Becks, Newcastle.

Champs is dark and smoky as you might expect. The big draw is the three huge screens and the satellite dish which brings in the games. You can call and ask if they will be showing the event which interests you. If they say yes, you hope that it will be on one of the big screens. If not, you get to watch your event on one of the many TVs scattered throughout the bar. It sort of operates as a semidemocracy—the most popular events get onto the big screens. The difference between Champs and other so-called sports bars is that Champs really knows how to operate their dish and keep everything running smoothly. Of course, this is Montreal, the ultimate hockey town, so hockey is king during the season, but many other events are also available. Soccer playoffs are pandemonium.

# Z DOVAL

Marie-Anne East (near de Bullion)
843-3390
Hours: 11 a.m.-10 p.m., except Sunday 8 a.m.-11 p.m.
Credit cards: Visa, MC, EnRoute
Licence: yes
Wheelchair access: yes
Reservations recommended week-ends

This popular neighbourhood Portuguese restaurant offers a small selection of grilled meat and fish at fantastic prices.

Vegetarians shouldn't bother coming here; it's heavy duty grilled meat and fish. All main dishes come with fries and salad. Portions are extremely generous. Main courses include: quail ($9.50), pork ($9), thick, juicy, perfectly grilled lamb chops (4 of them!) ($10), wonderfully fresh poached whiting drizzled with olive oil and vinegar ($10). The most popular dishes are the excellent grilled chicken ($8 piquant or not), and that quintessential Portuguese specialty, grilled sardines ($8.50). The fries are not the greatest so ask for a boiled potato, or stick to the crisp hot rolls which are plentiful. Black olives are complimentary. The flan ($2.50) is very good if you can manage it after the enormous main courses!

This is a busy place—people come from all over the city and the immediate neighbourhood. It's been around for more than 20 years, and it is owned and run by the Marques family (Antonio, and his wife Maria who is the chef). On Thursday-Saturday evenings there are South American guitarists. The small space is lively and convivial, even on week nights. Sunday mornings are for espresso ($1.50) and cappuccino ($2.50) and a neighbourly chat. They have a small selection of port. There are tablecloths and comfortable chairs; families and kids are welcome but you could certainly have an intimate dinner here too. Chez Doval gives excellent value and the food is very good.

# CHEZ GATSÉ

**317 Ontario East** (near Berri, métro Berri-UQAM)
985-2494
Hours: Tuesday-Thursday 11 a.m.-2:30 p.m.,
5:30 p.m.-9:30 p.m., Friday-Saturday 5 p.m.-10 p.m.,
Sunday 1 p.m.-9 p.m., closed Monday
Credit cards: Visa, MC, Interac
Licence: yes
Wheelchair access: no

Chez Gatsé is the only Tibetan restaurant in Montreal—
and a fine one it is!

The menu features authentic Tibetan homestyle comfort
food. Dishes are an eclectic mix of Indian/Chinese, with
subtle spicing, not hot and spicy as one might think. The
house salad ($2.75) is excellent, as is the lentil soup. Main
dishes include an interesting variety, including momos
(beef or vegetable dumplings $6.50-$7), tender beef or
chicken shapta ($7), pork chops Kongpo ($7.60), and
delicious noodle dishes ($4.50-$6.25). Specials change
daily and are $6.25 at lunch and $7.50 in the evening, including soup and beverage. Food is prepared without
preservatives or MSG. The salty Tibetan butter tea is a
curiosity in the West—an acquired taste.

Service is friendly and unobtrusive. Staff are all Tibetan
and are very pleased to explain to the uninitiated. There is
a pleasant terrace in good weather—somewhat stark, but
comfortable with trees, plants, and cats! The interior is
cozy— a very pleasant way to spend an evening out.

# CHEZ SOI

**421 Marie-Anne East** (near St-Denis, métro Mont-Royal)
847-7598
Hours: Monday-Friday 5 p.m.-7 p.m., closed Saturday
and Sunday
Credit cards: none
Licence: no
Wheelchair access: no

Chez Soi offers eclectic vegetarian fare at rock bottom prices on the Plateau.

The food here is wholly vegetarian. The menu, which is one choice each day, changes daily but menus for the week are posted outside the restaurant each Monday. The price is a fixed $4.75 for all you can eat, including dessert. The food is healthy and plentiful, including things like grains, fresh vegetables, pasta with vegetarian sauces, and salad with dressing. The food is delicious and well prepared by the owner/cook, Hélène, who uses lots of herbs and fresh ingredients. Desserts are healthy (i.e. less sweet and less rich) versions of cakes and such goodies as chocolate chip cookies. Water is the only beverage available. The food is delicious as well as being virtuous, and combinations are imaginative and tasty.

The restaurant is small, clean, comfortable, and casual. There are brightly painted chairs, small tables, and artwork on the walls. You pay at the counter and a friendly server gives you a huge plate of food. Diners help themselves from the water cooler and are asked to clear their own plates and place them in the sink. Chez Soi has been providing tasty and healthful food to the neighbourhood for about 10 years. Hélène's cooking comes from a lifetime of vegetarianism and her love of cooking. She makes it all work. This is a place where you can discover how delicious and appetizing healthy food can actually be!

# CHEZ TUNG

**288 Laurier** (near Park, métro Laurier, 51 bus)
3593 Appleton (near Plaza Côte-des-neiges,
métro Côte-des-Neiges, 165 bus)
278-6753; 735-1888
Hours: Monday-Friday 11:30 a.m.-10 p.m.; Saturday and
Sunday 4-l0 p.m.
Credit cards: Visa, MC, Amex, Interac, EnRoute
BYOB
Wheelchair access: no

This restaurant provides low-cost, quality Vietnamese food in a pleasant environment, with two locations.

The menu is the same in both locations and there are choices to meet all tastes. Soups ($1.75-$3) are varied and substantial. Four complete dinners are available for under $10/person (and four others between $10.50 and $15/person). Complete dinners include soup, imperial rolls, one or more main courses such as beef curry ($7.75), chicken with cherry sauce ($7.75), garlic shrimp ($9), rice, and almond cookies. The à la carte menu includes garlic beef ($6.25), Thai chicken ($5.75), shrimp with spicy sauce ($7). The daily specials provide soup, spring rolls, biscuits and tea, and include choices such as chicken with shrimps ($8.95) and grilled salmon with Tonkinese sauce ($8.75). The sauces are homemade by owner, Mme Pham, and they add a distinctive note to the food. Everything is fresh and tastes are authentic and delicious.

Mme Pham and her family opened on Appleton in 1982. The second location (1992) recently relocated to Laurier from Park Avenue. Both locations have lots of atmosphere and comfortable chairs, and are a good bet for a special intimate dinner on a budget. The restaurant is often busy so reservations are recommended. Chez Tung provides great food, excellent value, and it even has atmosphere. This is a real winner!

# COPOLI

**5181 de Maisonneuve West** (near Vendôme, métro Vendôme)
**4458 Ste-Catherine West**, (near Metcalfe, Westmount)
483-0000
Hours: Monday-Thursday 6 a.m.-11 p.m.;
Friday 6 a.m.-midnight; Saturday 9 a.m.-midnight;
and Sunday 9 a.m.-10 p.m.
Credit cards: none
Licence: Beer and wine
Wheelchair access: no

Copoli is famous for its oversize hamburgers—and they're delicious too. People bet on whether or not they can finish one!

Start with the basics. The Iranian flat bread for the burgers is made fresh daily very early in the morning (at both locations), large enough for the HUGE half pound of quality beef, grilled to juicy perfection. The daily pasta specials ($9.75—salad or soup and garlic bread) include a variety of fettuccine with sauces freshly made as you order, such as pesto rosso (chicken, sun-dried tomatoes, mushrooms, napped in a light tomato sauce with white wine), and the primavera (fresh basil and garden vegetables in a rosé sauce). The veal scallopini is $10.95 and is served with pasta, salad or soup, and garlic bread; the marinated grilled chicken is $7.95. All the specials include taxes.

The freshness of the food is what sets Copoli apart—even the tomato sauce is made from scratch, as is the pizza dough for the nine varieties of pizza offered.The daily soups ($2), made with real chicken stock include cream of carrot, dhal, and the delicious Persian-inspired osh made with turnips, cauliflower, and mung bean.

This friendly resto was started by the Motebassem family three years ago. They also own the branch on Ste-Catherine. Their recipes are unique and the burgers and pasta just don't get any better than this.

# COSMO FAMOUS SNACK BAR

**5843 Sherbrooke Street West** (near Regent, métro Vendôme, 105 bus)
486-3814
Hours: 7 a.m.-6 p.m., closed Monday
Credit cards: none
Licence: no
Wheelchair access: yes

Cosmo offers breakfast all day, and a few choice sandwiches in a funky NDG snack bar.

This is a specialty place if ever there was one. They specialize in breakfast any time of the day, and some selected sandwiches, but they also specialize in a relaxed and friendly atmosphere where both regulars and strangers feel equally at home. Breakfast combos include one egg with toast and two coffees ($2.25), two eggs with five slices of bacon or three sausages or ham or salami, with toast, home fries, and two coffees ($3.65, $5 for double meat portion). Eggs are cooked to perfection from long practice, and generous servings of home fries are unparalleled! A cheese sandwich is $1.25, and a bacon, lettuce and tomato (BLT) is a mere $2.50! The highly reputed "famous creation sandwich" ($3) includes eggs/ tomato/cheese/ham/bacon/salami, and is served with home fries! Hamburgers are also available ($2-$2.50).

Cosmos Koulakis has been the owner-manager-chef-waiter-dishwasher for 28 years. His son and wife also work in the business. There is a counter and, weather permitting, there are tables and chairs outside. This is a friendly and busy place with regulars who obviously love the place and feel at home there, but newcomers are very well received. The food is clearly cooked with love and it shows. The Cosmo experience is worth the trip, even from across town.

## CRISTAL DE SAIGON

**1068 St-Laurent Blvd**. (near la Gauchetière,
métro Place d'Armes or St-Laurent, 55 bus)
875-4275
Hours:11:30 a.m.-10 p.m.
Credit cards: none
Licence: no
Wheelchair access: no

Cristal de Saigon serves wonderful Vietnamese/Chinese soups that are one-bowl meals.

The menu offers 17 soups—so many it is sometimes hard to tell the difference between them! They are all tasty, well composed, and very generous as well as inexpensive ($3-$4.50). The best thing to do is just order whatever strikes your fancy on any particular day—you can't really go wrong choosing from among ingredients like BBQ pork, chicken, beef balls, shrimp, and noodles. The basic broth is fantastic to begin with, and can only improve with the addition of various meats, noodles, vegetables, and a final benediction of fresh mint or coriander. Nothing is overcooked or mushy, and it all comes together beautifully. The imperial rolls (two/$3) are perfect, as are the spring rolls (two/$3.20). If you don't want soup, the stewed beef with vegetables ($4.50) is recommended.

Run by a Vietnamese Chinese family, the Cristal de Saigon has been around for more than 12 years. It was one of the first Vietnamese soup places in town, and it is still one of the best. It's very clean with no décor to speak of. This is not a place to linger—there are almost always people waiting to be seated. The staff are friendly and the service is excellent. This is a place for Vietnamese comfort food. These one-bowl meals just make you feel good!

# DONG QUE

**1001 St-Laurent Blvd.** (near Viger, métro St-Laurent, 55 bus)
395-0529
Hours: 10 a.m.-10 p.m.
Credit cards: Visa, MC, Interac
Licence: wine & beer
Wheelchair access: no

This restaurant serves hearty Vietnamese family fare on the edge of Chinatown.

The menu is extensive and includes some Thai dishes, but the kitchen does Vietnamese cooking best. Many Vietnamese families share meals here as a profusion of heaping steaming dishes arrives at the larger tables. Soups are big and generous ($4-$5) with lots of fresh vegetables and plenty of meat. Spring rolls are large, crispy and delicious ($2.50-$3.50). The best bets are the set meals of Vietnamese specialties, Beef 7 dishes style ($16), and Beef 4 dishes style ($14)—several separate beef dishes. One-person portions are definitely generous enough for two. There are terrific lunch specials, 10 a.m.-3 p.m. ($4.95-$6.95 for Vietnamese complete meals). All portions are very generous and everything is cooked fresh. Chinese and Vietnamese beer are both available. Iced espresso ($1.50) made with condensed milk is a popular specialty.

The restaurant opened in December 1996. Nguyen Vien is the owner and Luong Giang Tan is manager—both have worked in local restaurants for the past 20 years. Decoration is minimal but not unpleasant. Tablecloths are plastic covered, and chairs are comfortable. There is seating for about 50 and everything can be easily re-arranged to accommodate larger groups. They hope to open the upstairs soon.

# ELIO PIZZERIA

**351 Bellechasse** (near Drolet, 55 bus)
276-5341
Hours: Monday-Friday noon-9 p.m., Tuesday-Thursday
noon-midnight, Friday-Saturday noon-2 a.m.,
Sunday noon-11 p.m.
Credit cards: Visa, MC, Interac
Licence: yes
Wheelchair access: no
Reservations required on weekends

This is the neighbourhood Italian restaurant most of us dream of but seldom find.

For many years Elio's has offered the very best homestyle Italian food at reasonable prices—the kind of comfort food your Italian grandmother might serve. It's neither nouvelle nor trendy—just delicious. The best thing to eat here is any kind of pasta *al forno* (in the oven)—a steaming hot plate of pasta oozing with melted cheeses and homemade sauce. Ahhh!!! The regular menu offers four different kinds (lasagna, ravioli, gnocchi, cannelloni $9-$9.75), but the daily specials usually include one as well, at a better price. Other pastas are good too, as are the homemade meatballs. The Italian-style pizza comes in a variety of combinations and sizes, all delicious. Portions are generous—no one leaves hungry. The menu includes a variety of other things but most people stick to the pizza and the pasta.

The restaurant started out as the proverbial hole-in-the-wall many years ago, but it simply had to expand. Although often crowded and busy, the quality of the food never suffers. There are banquet facilities upstairs (same food). Elio's does a big take-out business. Free parking is available across the street. This is a family business of the best kind, all the generations are involved, and Mama still rules the kitchen. The owners have supported a variety of amateur sports and the walls are festooned with plaques, photos, and pennants. Elio's is part of the neighbourhood—aren't we lucky!

# ENCORE UNE FOIS

**351 Prince Albert** (Westmount, near Sherbrooke
and Victoria, métro Vendôme, 24 bus)
488-3390
Hours: Sunday-Friday 11 a.m.-11 p.m., Saturday-
Sunday 10 a.m.-11 p.m.
Credit cards: Visa, MC, Amex
Licence: BYOB
Wheelchair access: no

Encore une fois is a successful Westmount neighbourhood
restaurant with great homestyle food and a funky atmosphere.

There is a subdued healthy food feeling here, but it is
not overdone, and the emphasis is on good fare. (The
drinking water is filtered through activated carbon filters.)
The menu features a variety of fresh sandwiches ($3.95-
$4,95), including roast beef ($3.95) and goat cheese
($3.95). The sandwich platters ($5.95-$6.95) are very
generous—two open face sandwiches, sprouts, grated
cheese, and carrot salad, with garnishes! There are fresh
juices, and the desserts are truly homemade treasures (rice
pudding $2.75, apple pie $3.25, opéra cake $3.95). Salad
dressings (five varieties) are a house specialty. There is
an evening special every day for $9.95, including soup,
salad and coffee, and a lunch menu for $6.95, including
soup, salad, and main course. There is a special brunch
menu on weekends. Everything is fresh, tasty, well put
together, and excellent value.

This is a very pleasant place, high ceilings and natural
light, with small tables, wooden chairs, and counter stools
at the window. It's a little cramped but very congenial,
with vintage wooden commercial refrigerators and a
beautiful old cash register. There are a few old signs, and
one corner wall is covered with Pine Valley Camp
memorabilia (owner Leonard Baltin attended). Staff is
young, competent, and helpful. Encore une fois is a place
to come back to again and again.

# ERNIE & ELLIE'S PLACE

**6900 Decarie** (in Decarie Square Shopping Centre, main floor, métro Namur, 17,166 bus)

344-4444

Hours: Monday-Thursday 11 a.m.-2:30 p.m., 5 p.m.-9:30 p.m., closed on Friday at 2 p.m. (winter), and 3 p.m. (summer), Sunday 11 a.m.-10 p.m., closed on major Jewish holidays

Credit cards: Visa, MC, Interac

Licence: yes

Wheelchair access: yes


This Kosher (certified MK by the Jewish Community Council of Montreal) restaurant in Decarie Square Shopping Centre serves excellent Canadian and Chinese food, and does catering too!

The best bet at Ernie & Ellie's is a selection from the dinner specials ($10) which include a choice of soup, main course, side dishes, dessert, and beverage. There are always two choices, one Canadian and one Chinese. Soup choices are eclectic—bean and barley, chicken noodle, cabbage, hot and sour, mushroom, egg drop and won ton. They're homemade and really good. The chicken dishes are always tasty, and the Chinese selections include garlic beef spare ribs and General Tao chicken. Some of the dishes are unique and interesting, Chinese cuisine adapted to meet kosher dietary laws. The regular table d'hôte menu ranges from $10.95-$16.95. Vegetarian and fish dishes are available, but no dairy products are available in the restaurant, a boon to the lactose-intolerant. Steak, Cajun chicken sandwich and breaded veal cutlets are among the menu choices. Lunch brings 11 choices of Canadian and Chinese meals, everything included, for $5.50.

This is the former Deli Peking Kosher Chinese restaurant, with expanded premises and menu. It is Montreal's best Kosher eatery and is a major caterer to boot. The space is pleasant, an oasis in the rather grey shopping mall. Staff are helpful and courteous. The food is not just kosher, it's GOOD!

# FARROUJ

**3575 Park Avenue** (in Galeries du Parc, at Prince-Arthur, 80 bus)
285-8729
Hours: Monday-Friday 10:30 a.m.-8 p.m., Saturday-Sunday 11 a.m.-5 p.m.
Credit cards: Visa, Interac
Licence: yes
Wheelchair access: yes

This fast food place in Galeries du Parc serves Middle Eastern food, including great falafel, with a few special touches like wonderful fresh tropical juices!

The menu includes very good renditions of shish-taouk ($3.45/$7), shawarma ($3.25/$6.50), hummous ($2) and excellent baba ghannouj ($2). Then there is the falafel! Good falafel is hard to find—and this is a very unlikely place—the mall in Galéries du Parc, huddled up against the movie theatre. Why is it so good here? It's from scratch ("no mix"), and served with fresh mint. There are falafel sandwiches after 3 p.m. for only $1.75 with all the fixings. The soup is made fresh every day ($1.25 including pita). Vine leaves are made in-house daily ($2.50/6 pieces) and they are stuffed with rice, parsley and a secret ingredient. The fresh fruit juices are extraordinarily good and very popular, especially with the after workout crowd from the mall's health club. The fave is the pineapple, orange, banana, mango combo ($2/12 oz, $3/16 oz).

Farrouj changed owners in 1996 but current owners Mohamad and Rana Alameddine and Maumtaz Kabbara have maintained the fine quality—at rock bottom prices. Farrouj is more popular at lunch than at dinner—it's a little hard to come up with atmosphere in an underground mini-mall—but the food here is worth the trip, whatever the time of day. You can sit down to enjoy the food, or make it take-out and nibble your falafel sandwich as you amble over to the video store.

# GALAXIE DINER

**4801 St-Denis** (Gilford, métro Laurier)
499-9711
Hours: Monday-Wednesday 7 a.m.-10 p.m., Thursday-Saturday 7 a.m.-11 p.m., Sunday 7 a.m.-10 p.m.
Credit cards: Visa, MC,
Licence: no
Wheelchair access: yes, but not washroom

Galaxie Diner updates 1950s diner style food for the 90s, and moves it smack dab to the middle of St-Denis.

The food here is basic and varied. Breakfasts are good and plentiful. Just about everything else on the menu comes with thin cut homemade fries and delicious cole-slaw. Hamburgers are juicy and generous patties in a good bun, and a number of variations are available, including the special (cream cheese, mushrooms, lettuce, and tomato, $7.25). The menu also includes the buffalo burger with mozzarella, ($8.88), a large club sandwich ($8.97), a chili dog ($5.24), fish and chips ($7.33) or the classic hot chicken sandwich ($7.34). A children's menu is $4.49 for a hamburger, hot dog or grilled cheese (served in a nifty take-away cardboard car serving dish) with juice/milk and fries. There are sundaes and other soda fountain desserts and drinks when you want to blow the works.

Galaxie is a real live diner, decorated appropriately with pink and stainless steel, comfortable booths, 50s-style arborite table tops and bathroom-tile floor. The waitresses wear blue uniforms with little white caps, and carry a metal change dispenser. The juke box includes "Love Me Tender," and "Chantilly Lace." The diner was moved to this spot from the U.S. and it opened in March 1993. It's now a popular neighbourhood fixture for young and old. Despite the potential for hype and kitsch, Galaxie delivers decent basic food with a menu updated for the 90s, at reasonable prices. And it's fun too!

# GENUINE RESTAURANT

**5487 Victoria** (near Dupuis, Côte-St-Catherine métro, 124 bus)
738-3881
Hours: Noon-1 a.m. (sometimes earlier, call ahead)
Credit cards: none
Licence: yes
Wheelchair access: yes

Sri Lankan food is the specialty in this family-run restaurant, and take-out is the best bet.

The kitchen is basically Sri Lankan with a mix of other influences—the husband is Tamil but he has worked in Mexican restaurants, the wife is Indian, the neighbourhood is West Indian. The food is eclectic but GOOD! Sri Lankan dishes are similar to Southern Indian food. Main dishes are $4-$7 and portions are huge. Things you won't find elsewhere include: the exquisite Kottu roti ($6), chopped up roti bread with onions, chilis, eggs, and beef curry, as well as Masala dosa ($4.50) a huge crepe filled with curried veggies and served with chutney, both dishes come with sambar, a terrific vegetable lentil stew. Service is slow because all main dishes are made to order. There are also biryanis and curries.

They have been open for four years and often there is just one person cooking, serving and waiting table. This is a very tiny and unadorned space, with room for less than 20 people, but most people come for take-out. What matters here is the food. Call in your order ahead and pick it up. You won't be disappointed—the Genuine has genuinely good stuff!

# GRANO

**3647 St-Laurent Blvd**.(near Pine, métro St-Laurent, 24, 29, 55, 144 bus)
840-9000, grano@odyssee.net
Hours: noon-midnight (later if they are busy, a little earlier if not)
Credit cards: Visa, MC, Amex, Interac
Licence: yes
Wheelchair access: yes but it could get difficult in places

Grano is a trendy St-Laurent sandwich emporium which serves fresh-fresh-fresh sandwiches and fruit drinks, as well as decadent desserts.

You can pick and choose your sandwich combos (breads and fillings) here. Someone has done the math and apparently there are 1,382,400 sandwich possibilities. They have wisely chosen to use a variety of yummy Première Moisson breads. Good bets are the fagotto (baked bread bundle) prosciutto/bocconcini/grilled mushrooms ($8.95) served with a beverage and salad or fries. The Diabolique ($6.66) combines Genoa salami with grilled mushrooms, Swiss cheese and Lucifer sauce, served with fries or salad. The menu presents 25 sandwich combos with fresh fruit garnishes, all of which are good. Fries are oven baked and they can sometimes be soggy, but at least you can feel virtuous about them. Dessert cakes are from Dan's Delight and they're exquisite—although you can't feel virtuous about them! Fruit drinks ($3.75, more for ice cream and alcohol combos) are so good the only problem is to choose which ones you can't have.

Anthony and Pino DiIoia (twin brothers) opened Grano in the fall of 1996. They had previously been involved with franchises but wanted a place of their own, so they went back to their Italian roots for inspiration. The long narrow space is interestingly organized and the minimalist design has won several awards. There were some service glitches when they first opened but these have been sorted out. This is a hip spot that serves good food.

# L'HARMONIE D'ASIE

**65 Duluth East** (near Coloniale, métro St-Laurent, 55 bus)
289-9972
Hours: 5 p.m.-10 p.m.
Credit cards: Visa,MC
Licence: yes
Wheelchair access: no

L'Harmonie d'Asie serves delicious Vietnamese food in a charming spot on the Plateau.

They have a good selection of beef, fish, seafood, and vegetarian dishes. Beef sauté with vegetables is $6.50, beef curry is $6.95, chicken with lemon grass is $6.95, fish curry is $7.50, and crispy grilled duck with rice is $9.95. Chicken with ginger is a great bargain at $6.95. Prices range generally between $6.50 and $10. All dishes come with rice and salad. The imperial roll ($1.40) is homemade and vegetarian. Portions are extremely generous—you may not be able to finish. Ask for a doggie bag—the leftovers make a great lunch. Asparagus and crab soup ($1.95) is a house specialty and is very flavourful. Jasmine tea is $1.50

The locale is small and charming—a good spot to spend a pleasant evening without breaking the budget. Food presentation and service are fine and the staff are friendly. Sitting by the window gives you a great view of the passing parade on Duluth. This is a very popular neighbourhood spot, with lots of regulars.

# IZA

**1001 Ontario East** (near St-Timothée, métro Berri-UQAM, 125 bus)
890-1015
Hours: noon-midnight
Licence: yes
Wheelchair access: 1 step

This bright and cheerful restaurant on the edge of the Gay Village offers good Mexican food and also does catering.

The menu includes Mexican specialties (some vegetarian versions), tacos ($6.95), chili con carne ($6.95), burritos ($7.95), enchiladas ($8.25, $9.25), fajitas ($9.95), nachos (with cheese $4.25, with chili $5.25), ceviche of shrimp ($5.75). The daily specials are a good deal ($6.95-$11.95) and include a main dish, guacamole, coffee, and dessert. Specials can include enchiladas, tacos and rice and other Mexican delights. Salsas have a warm glow—they don't knock your socks off. On Sundays the menu often includes a typical Dominican Republic specialty—Soncochos, a stew of chicken, pork, and plantain. They serve breakfast on the weekend, including bagels with cream cheese and fruit ($4.95, with salmon $6.95), and huevos rancheros ($5.25). Lunch specials ($6.99) are also available.

Chef Placido Sims from the Dominican Republic, and his wife, are the owners. Iza began as a catering business. The restaurant is spacious and bright with colourful Mexican décor and a relaxed atmosphere. The chairs are comfortable and there are windows on two sides. Kids are definitely welcome. Service is friendly but it can be a bit slow. The time passes quickly if you munch on the complimentary tortillas and salsa, and sip sangria ($12.95/litre) or Corona beer ($3.50). On a blustery winter day this is almost as good as a trip to a warm, sunny spot.

# JARDIN DU CARI (CARIBBEAN CURRY GARDEN)

**21 St-Viateur West**   (near St-Laurent, 55 bus)
495-0565
Hours: Monday-Friday noon-10 p.m., Saturday,
Sunday 5 p.m.-10 p.m.
Credit cards: none
Licence: yes
Wheelchair access: no

Everything is prepared fresh to order in this unpretentious Guyanese/Caribbean/Indian eat-in or take-out restaurant on the Plateau.

Roti is the specialty of the house at Curry Garden—shrimp ($5.50), mutton ($3.75), boneless chicken ($3.95—one of the most popular), chickpea and potato ($3.50). These are arguably the best roti in town. No only are they great, they come with a wonderful house sauce (smooth and very hot) which is homemade from scotch bonnets, the hottest peppers on the planet, smooth, tasty, and redolent with lemon. This sauce is much more than just hot, it is absolutely wonderful. Mutton or chicken curry ($5 with rice) is rich and flavourful, and patties are $1 each. Potato balls (4/$1) are crispy delights. Be sure to add the house sauce. Peanut punch is $1.75 and Caribbean soft drinks are available for $1.50. There are bottle openers on the tables.

This homey and unpretentious place has about 20 comfortable seats but more than half the business is take-out. This is a family business. Rita Dommer (whose father taught her to cook) and husband Singh opened Curry Garden in July 1997 with the help of a brother and sister-in law. This is their first restaurant and they both cook, although it is usually Rita who greets customers. The menu is straightforward and the variety is not huge but the food is very fresh and flavour combinations are great. They will cater for groups and are open to doing special orders. These people know how to cook!

# JAVA U

**1455 Guy** (Corner of de Maisonneuve and Guy,
métro Guy-Concordia, 165)
Hours: Monday-Friday 6 a.m.-11 p.m., Saturday-
Sunday, 8 a.m.-7 p.m.
Credit cards: none
Licence: no
Wheelchair access: no

This downtown coffee bar serves salad and panini in a
tiny crowded space with great atmosphere.

Green Mountain coffee from Vermont in all possible
incarnations, and fancy teas are front and centre in this
small place, but the good food is what makes it really work.
The panini ($2.99, $3.99 with salad) is very popular,
including La Bamba (tuna, tomato, mozzarella), Club Med
(feta, sun dried tomato, tomato, olives and capers), and
Om (tofu, ginger). Fresh pasta salad ($2) and homemade
soup ($2.25) change daily. There is good vegetarian ($5)
or fish sushi ($6). Desserts change regularly and can
include brownies ($1.75), lemon turnover ($1.25), fancy
cakes like opéra ($3.50). They also serve excellent cookies
(85¢) and muffins ($1), and croissant ($1.25). Fresh fruit
drinks or hot apple cider ($2.25) are popular.

Innovative owners Asher (formerly in real estate) and
Ron (previously worked in delis) opened this place in 1996
replacing the Laura Secord which had been on this corner
forever—a sign of changing tastes. Staff are friendly and
efficient. Tables, chairs, counters and stools are crammed
into the tiny space, but the atmosphere is convivial.
Background music is usually wonderful jazz. In good
weather people spill out onto sidewalk tables. Evenings
are quieter than days and lingering is the norm. They have
Lactaid milk available for the lactose-intolerant (add 65¢).
Java U is an interesting alternative to fast food chains—a
downtown coffee bar with good food at reasonable prices.

# JUST NOODLES

**2061 Ste-Catherine West** (near Fort, Guy-Concordia, or Atwater métro, 15 bus)
989-5826
Hours: 11:30 a.m.-10:30 p.m.
Credit cards: none
Licence: no
Wheelchair access: a small stair

This simple noodle emporium offers comfort food— fresh noodles in a pleasant, unpretentious atmosphere.

Just Noodles offers a little more variety than just noodles, but noodles are clearly the specialty, and what they do best. The noodle dishes are a meal in a bowl (either soup or noodles with various fixings) and the prices range from \$4.50-\$6.50. The menu (in Chinese, French, and English) offers 38 noodle selections. The choice includes seafood noodle soup (\$5.50), excellent Satay seafood rice noodle (\$6.50), and very good phad Thai (\$6.50). Spicy items are indicated. The menu also includes other items such as spring rolls (\$2.50), chicken with basil and fried rice (\$6), rice with spiced bean curd (\$6), but almost everyone orders the noodle dishes. The food is extremely fresh and made to order right in front of you. Portions are generous and tastes are clear and delicious, although some selections can be a little bland—the perfect comfort food if that is what you're after.

This noodle shop, owned by four Chinese partners, opened in July 1997 and it's a welcome addition to the restaurant scene. The spotlessly clean kitchen is open and it's fun to watch the food being prepared. They use MSG but will leave it out if you ask. There are lineups at lunch but it's worth the wait. You get real value here—prices even include the tax!

# MA-AM-M BOLDUC!

**4351 Delorimier** (near Marie-Anne, métro Papineau,
10 bus)
527-3884
Hours: Monday-Wednesday 7 a.m.-9 p.m., Thursday-Friday
7 a.m.-10 p.m., Saturday 8 a.m.-10 p.m., Sunday 9 a.m.-
9 p.m.,10 p.m. closing every day during the summer
Credit cards: Visa, Interac
Licence: wine and beer
Wheelchair access: no

All-day breakfast and Québécois specialties are offered
in style in this neighbourhood restaurant with a long-standing and proud pedigree.

This is the place for the very best Québécois comfort
food. Breakfast items are offered all day—two eggs, toast,
and coffee ($2.80), French toast with fruit, maple syrup
and coffee ($4.30), 2 eggs, bacon, sausage, baked beans,
fruit, cretons, potatoes, coffee ($5.95). There are also
traditional dishes like shepherd's pie (pâté chinois $6.25),
meatball stew (ragoût de boulettes $6.75), a selection of
terrific poutines ($3.75-$8.95) and several excellent
hamburgers ($2.60-$6.25). The daily special is $6.95 at
lunch and $8.95-$11.95 at dinner. Everything is so good
it's hard to choose. The cheesecake is simply sublime,
and the pudding chômeur is good enough to get your
grandmother worried! Belle Geule draft is $2.70 for a 12-
oz-glass and $6 for a 30-oz-pitcher.

The history of this restaurant is proudly printed on the
cover of the delightful menu. Madame Bolduc opened a
very popular corner restaurant in 1972 on the site of her
father's grocery store. In 1987 the torch was passed to
Gilles Couture and eventually to his son Martin. Lucky
for us. The atmosphere is cozy and comfortable, and kids
are very welcome. The food is great, and it is virtually
impossible to spend more than $10 for a meal. This place
is a quintessential Cheap Thrill—not to be missed!

# MANZO PIZZA

**1033-90th Avenue** (near Newman, métro Angrignon, 106 bus)
366-1319
Hours: Monday-Wednesday 11 a.m.-1 a.m., Thursday-Saturday 11 a.m.-2 p.m., Sunday 3 p.m.-1 a.m.
Credit cards: none
Licence: no
Wheelchair access: yes

Wonderful pizza and Italian submarines are the pride and joy of this pizzeria in Ville LaSalle.

Manzo's pizza was voted by radio station CJAD listeners as the Best Pizza in Montreal in 1996. The sauce is made fresh every morning, and it is really good. The Chef's special pizza (9" $6.95, 10" $8.95, 12" $11.95, 14" $15.50, 16" $18.95) comes all dressed with bacon and smoked meat—delicious and amazingly, not greasy. It's even good as leftovers the next morning. The submarines are made from the restaurant's own fresh dough, and baked on the spot. The Manzo special ($7.50 for 10", $8.50 for 14") combines steak, pepperoni, Italian sausage, mushrooms, peppers, onions, and cheese and it's a challenge to finish it. There is a vegetarian submarine available as well ($6.25, $7.25). The freshly daily house dressing adds a special touch to the juicy subs. They also serve a selection of pastas ($5.95-$7.50) and there are 16 daily lunch specials for $5.95.

This treasure is tucked away near LaSalle's Whisky Trench, and it has been part of the community since 1986. Proud owner-chef Steve Triantopolous runs the kitchen and exerts serious quality control. He makes the sauce and the house dressing personally and nothing leaves the kitchen without his approval. Take-out and delivery are very popular and pick-up gets you a 15% discount. This is a very popular spot and its reputation is well deserved.

# MAZURKA

**64 Prince-Arthur East** (near St-Laurent Blvd., métro
Sherbrooke, 24, 55, or 144 bus)
844-3539
Hours: 11:30 a.m-midnight
Licence: yes
Credit cards: Visa, MC, Amex
Wheelchair access: terrace and front section OK, but not
washrooms

The Mazurka serves Polish comfort food and is one of the
best deals in town.

This is how your mom would cook if she were Polish.
The $5 special ($5.75 after 5 p.m., and all day Friday and
Saturday) features pirogis and meat or cheese blintzes,
potato pancakes, or Polish sausage. The low price even
includes great homemade soup, and a beverage. It's
impossible to spend a lot of money here, even with the à
la carte specialties such as wiener schnitzel, green pepper
steak, and the perennial Mazurka favourite, goulash.
Everything tastes like mother's home cooking and portions
are generous. Desserts are crème caramel, cakes, and cheesecake. The wines are available at close to cost price.

The Mazurka is a local institution. Stanislaw Mazurek
opened the restaurant in 1952 on St-Laurent, and it moved
to its present location in 1964 amid the plumbing and
sandal shops. Now part of a trendy strip, it is run by
Mazurek's daughter Josephine, her husband Jesse, and
their son Mark. The Mazurka "family" includes servers
Mike, Zutka, Vickie, and Nina, who have been there for
decades, as have many of the patrons. There is a terrace
section which is available in good weather. The
atmosphere is informal and friendly, with folksy paintings
of the old country on the walls. Service is friendly and
extremely efficient. These people have been doing this
for a long time and they know how to do it extremely
well! Mazurka is one of the best deals in town.

## MCKIBBINS PUB

**1426 Bishop** (near Ste-Catherine, métro Guy-Concordia, 15 bus)
288-1580
Hours: 11 a.m.-3 p.m. (food served until 10 p.m.)
Licence: yes
Wheelchair access: no

McKibbins is a typical Irish pub with all the trimmings, including very good food.

The menu here complements the bar, of course; it's small but interesting, and the food is prepared with care and skill. The house specialties are Irish stew ($6.75) prepared with lamb as it should be, fish and chips ($6.75), hamburgers and a club sandwich made with blue cheese. French fries ($2) are especially good. There are homemade sausage rolls ($5.75) and a terrific steak and kidney pie ($7.95) with delicate homemade crust and a savoury filling. The shepherd's pie is very good. Portions are generous. Sunday brunch (11 a.m.-2 p.m.) features a Celtic harpist. The winter menu includes homemade soda bread which is cooked in the fireplace. There are 16 imported beers on tap and a good selection of single malt scotch. Irish sports are available live via satellite. The Speakeasy cigar lounge is downstairs.

McKibbins is in one of the old greystone houses which still remain downtown and the atmosphere is warm, friendly, and inviting—a home away from home. They opened in August 1997 but it feels like they have been here forever! Dean McKibbin and Rick Fon own the business, and Julie is the very competent chef. Staff are friendly and helpful, and Irish bands provide entertainment—the monthly schedule is posted at the door. This is a very pleasant and affordable downtown spot, and the food is really good.

# LE MEDITERRANÉEN

**3857 St-Denis** (near Roy, métro Sherbrooke, 144 bus)
843-5028
Hours: 11 a.m.-11 p.m.
Credit cards: Visa, MC
Licence: yes
Wheelchair access: one step at street level, bathrooms OK

This Tunisian restaurant on St-Denis offers fresh and flavourful food and an extensive salad bar.

The menu is varied, with several lamb dishes. They also serve very good couscous and some vegetarian dishes. If you dine before 8 p.m. those dishes at $8.75 drop to $5.75 and up, including a trip to the salad bar, which features more than 40 different salads and fixings (olives, chick peas, sunflower seeds, etc.). The specials include pita and rolls, and a dessert counter with a selection of baklavas, cakes, and fresh fruit. Coffee is extra ($1.50). The assiette de mechoui ($8.95) includes rice and two vegetables, served with tender, succulent, garlicky lamb. Classic briks ($8.95-$9.95) are crisp and wonderful. The lamb brochette special in the evening is $8.95 including fries. Lunch specials ($5.75-$6.75) include lamb brochette, couscous, and mussels. The sangria ($14.95/pitcher) is good, with lots of fruit. Beer is $7.95 for a half pitcher and $14.95 for a whole pitcher.

This is a family-run restaurant. There are about a dozen tables, and the interior is cool blue. The TV features belly dancers and music, adding an exotic Middle Eastern ambiance. Service is attentive and friendly. Clientèle includes children and students. The atmosphere is pleasant and comfortable.

# AU MESSOB D'OR

**5690 Monkland** (near Harvard, métro Villa-Maria, 1
bus)
488-8620
Hours: Tuesday-Sunday 5 p.m.-10:30 p.m., closed Monday
Credit cards: Visa, MC
Licenced: yes
Wheelchair access: no, except for outside patio

This restaurant brings centuries old Ethiopian cooking
traditions to the heart of NDG—for under $10!

A subtle blending of spices, herbs, and red pepper go
into the making of delicious "wats", sauces served with
meat, poultry, grains or vegetables. The yedoro wat ($10)
is spiced chicken simmered with onions and berbère/red
pepper sauce. Lega tibs ($9) is sautéed lamb or beef with
green peppers. The vegetarian mixed plates ($7-8.50) are
a combination of dishes including lentils in berbère sauce,
chick pea purée with vegetables, or cold vegetable salad
with lemon and oil dressing. Each dish on the menu is
delicately spiced and has its own unique flavour.

Au Messob d'Or introduces us to the communal eating
style of Ethiopia. The food is placed on large platters lined
with injera, a flat bread which has a slight sourdough flavour.
Pieces of the bread are torn off with the fingers and used
to scoop up the thick sauces. The pièce de résistance is
eating the delicious sauce-soaked injera that remains after
everything else has been eaten. A perfect conclusion to
the meal is tea with cloves and cardamom ($1.75).

This is a tranquil and relaxed place, where food and
tradition are respected. The service is attentive and
friendly, and staff are pleased to explain Ethiopian
traditions, even on weekends when they are quite busy.
The restaurant was opened by three Ethiopians in December 1991. A pleasant terrace is available in good weather.

# LA METROPOLE

**1409 St-Marc** (near Ste-Catherine, métro Guy-Concordia)
932-3403
Hours: 11 a.m.-11 p.m.
Credit cards: none
Licence: yes
Wheelchair access: yes

This restaurant is run by two sisters, and offers Russian and European specialties on a budget, in an elegant atmosphere.

The table d'hôte ($6.25, $8.25, $11.95) is offered 11 a.m.-5 p.m. weekdays and is very good value for Russian and European dishes. At other times the menu offers good homemade soup ($3.25) which can be combined with some of the Russian specialties such as vareniky ($6.85) and pirozhki ($4.45)—especially good dumplings stuffed with meat and mushrooms or potatoes and apple, or blinchiki—crepes stuffed with meat or cheese ($4.25)—which are served with vegetables. The chicken legs stuffed with mushrooms ($7.95) are excellent. Garnishes are fresh and appetizing throughout. The salmon steak ($9.25) is outstanding. Fries are fresh and crisp. Sandwiches ($3.55-$5.75) and salads ($3.25-$7.75 for a fine salade Niçoise) are also available. The Napoleon cake or sour cream cake are wonderful, particularly good with Russian tea ($1.15).

Two Russian sisters Lydia (out front) and Wolia Khusid (the chef) opened this stylish restaurant in 1997. The décor is elegant and there are nice touches like fresh flowers, and live Russian music on week-ends. This is a great place for a special lunch downtown or an intimate evening out.

## MOULES & CIE

**77 Pine Avenue East** (near de Bouillon, métro St-Laurent, 55 bus)
842-0582 (fax 842-3149)
Hours: Monday-Thursday11 a.m.- 10 p.m., Friday 11-11, Sunday 4 p.m.-10 p.m.
Credit cards: Visa, MC, Interac
Licence: yes
Wheelchair access: no

This comfortable fish and seafood bistro is connected to Waldman's (they have the same owner, La Mer) and it has the freshest fish in town.

All you can eat mussels ($8.95) are always available. Plump and juicy, they're available in nine different styles. The two most popular choices are with oriental sauce or Mediterranean style. There is also the Catch of the Day ($8.95-$11.95—the higher prices tend to be on the weekend), which include soup or salad and coffee. These can include house specialties, kingfish Island style and Cajun-style red snapper, or fish brochettes. The fries are excellent—hot, crisp, cooked to perfection, and served with mayonnaise. Determined landlubbers can order chicken breast with lemon butter ($9.95) or steak and fries ($11.95), but why bother. Lunch specials are available for $5.95. The fish is incredibly fresh and cooked beautifully with wonderful accents.

This fish and seafood bistro (completely renovated and a change of management in early 1997) is the perfect spot for a family dinner or for a special evening. There are romantic lace café curtains, and comfy high-backed chairs. Every morning, manager Michel Fournier consults with the manager of Waldman's, Miguel (he's been there for more than 25 years), to find the very best and freshest fish. They turn it over to chef Hélin (born in Guadaloupe and trained in France), who knows *exactly* what to do with it. This is a real treasure!

# MR. STEER

**1198 Ste-Catherine West** (near Drummond, métro Peel, 15 bus)
866-3233
Hours: 7 a.m.-11 p.m.
Credit cards: Visa, MC
Licence: yes (beer and wine)
Wheelchair access: yes

Jimmy Gaspar, owner of Mr. Steer has been serving burgers and Suzy Q fries to Montrealers for over 40 years from this downtown location. Mr. Steer must be doing something right!

Every day, all day, there is a special at Mr. Steer for $5.99, including salad, fries, and beverage. There are two choices available daily from among 1/4 BBQ chicken, or Steerburger, or Mr. Frankfurter or chili. There are also good steaks at Mr. Steer. The Combo ($8.95) includes a Mister Steerburger and grilled chicken breast on a roll with salad and fries or baked potato. But what is really special here are the burgers and the fries. The burgers have often won popularity contests over the years, and they are thick, juicy, and delicious. Only fresh meat is used, never frozen. The standard Mr. Steerburger is $5.25 including Suzy Q fries and a generous bowl of salad, but additional fixings like bacon and cheese are also available. The Suzy Q fries are the pride of the house: very thin, curly, and fried to crispy perfection. Pies and total blowout soda fountain desserts are delicious—banana split ($5.95), sundaes ($3.85), and a brownie with hot fudge sauce and ice cream ($4.15).

Mr. Steer is like an old-fashioned diner—comfortable and very good at what it does. It can get very busy here on nights when there is an event at the Molson Centre.

# OKAMBO

**1301 Ontario East** (near de la Visitation, métro Berri-UQAM, 125 bus)
523-8754
Hours: Monday-Friday 11 a.m.-11 p.m., Saturday 2 p.m.-11 p.m., closed Sunday
Credit cards: Visa, Amex, Interac
Licenced: yes
Wheelchair access: entrance OK, washrooms a problem

This Eritrean/Ethiopian restaurant serves an eclectic mix of authentic Eritrean specialties and French food in a relaxed but very pleasant neighbourhood restaurant.

The authentic Eritrean specialties share the menu with equally authentic French crêpes. Eritrean food is usually served on a plate of injera (flat bread) on which food is spread. Pieces of injera are used to scoop up the food. The wat dishes ($8.95-$9.50) are generous and include choices of beef, chicken or lamb with rich sauce. The tibbsi is savoury sautéed beef ($9.50) or lamb ($10.50) with ginger garlic and onions. An interesting selection of vegetarian dishes is also available ($6.95). French crêpe choices include mushroom/béchamel ($6.95), campagnarde (fresh tomatoes, goat cheese and thyme, $7.95), and excellent dessert crêpes ($2.50-$4.95), with fillings such as chocolate, strawberries, ice cream, peaches, ricotta, and nuts. Draft Griffon beer goes very well with the food and is very affordable ($2.75/10-oz-glass, $7.95/32-oz-pitcher, $12.95/60-oz-pitcher). There are lunch specials for $7.99 and $9.99

The restaurant is owned by Sam Tewoldé and Geneviève Portanelli. He is Eritrean and she is French. It is a lively, warm, and welcoming place with bright colours, Eritrean motifs, and pleasant lighting. Some Friday evenings during the winter there is live West African music. Kids are welcome. There's something for everyone in this wonderful cultural mix!

## LA PARYSE

**302 Ontario East** (near Sanguinet, métro Berri-UQAM)
842-2040
Hours: Monday 11 a.m.-9:30 p.m., Tuesday-Friday 11 a.m.-
11 p.m., Saturday-Sunday 2 p.m.-10 p.m.
Credit cards: Visa, MC, Interac
Licence: beer and wine

La Paryse is often credited with serving the best hamburgers in town. They also serve delicious soup, sandwiches, and desserts.

The restaurant is small and often crowded (especially
5:30-7:30 p.m. on weekends when there is frequently a
lineup). They do not take reservations. The atmosphere is
friendly and informal, and service is efficient. Hamburgers
(regular $4.55) come with mozzarella, tomato, mush-
rooms, pickle, onion, lettuce, mayonnaise, and dijon
mustard. The "Special" hamburger ($5.25) comes with
cream cheese and bacon and is especially good. Fries
($1.95/$2.50) are homemade and delicious. Excellent
vegetable soup ($2.25) is also available. Portions are very
generous. Desserts include cakes ($2.95) and Bilboquet
ice cream and sherbet. Espresso and cappuccino are available at reasonable prices. In addition to the regular menu,
specials ($7.25) are available from 11 a.m.-3 p.m. Mon-
day-Friday, and at other times they are $8.25.

Everything at La Paryse is done with a special touch,
and with more care and attention than one might expect.
Although it bills itself as a snack bar, it is anything but
mundane. La Paryse offers simple food prepared extremely
well. You will find yourself going back again and again.

# PATTAYA

**5014 Park Avenue** (near Laurier, 80 or 51 bus)
Telephone: 277-4673
Hours: Monday-Friday 11:30 a.m.-11 p.m., Saturday-Sunday,
5 p.m.-11 p.m.
Credit cards: Visa, MC, Interac
Licence: yes
Wheelchair access: yes

Pattaya serves wonderful, yet affordable Thai food in a
warm and welcoming restaurant on Park Avenue.

All dishes include a spring roll and rice. Portions are
very generous (you will probably take home a doggie bag).
Choices include such house special delights as beef in
savoury green curry sauce with coconut milk and basil
($9.95), chicken with lots of rich peanut sauce, and very
crispy spinach ($8.95). Ingredients are extremely fresh
and the food covers the whole gamut of lightly spiced to
highly spiced. No MSG is used in the kitchen. Vegetarian
choices ($5.50-$6.50) are interesting. Most dishes are
$8.95-$9.95 but a few with seafood are a little more expensive. There is a lunch special for $5.95, including soup
and tea. Complete take-out meals for two ($15.95-$16.95)
or three ($20.95-$26.95) are also available and delivery
is free with a minimum $12 order.

Owner-chef Feng Yeming set up here after working at
the Sawatdee. He is amenable to special requests and
thrives on creating subtle mixtures of flavours and textures
which tickle both the palate and the imagination. He
concentrates on the natural flavours of the food and they
come through loud and clear in all his cooking. Take-out
and delivery are very popular (10% discount). This is an
attractive and welcoming restaurant, where it is a pleasure
to come alone, with kids, or for a leisurely evening with
friends.

# PEEL PUB

**1107 Ste-Catherine West** (near Peel, métro Peel, 15 bus)
870 de Maisonneuve East (near St-Hubert, métro Berri-UQAM, 15 bus)
844-6769; 849-8715
Hours: 7 a.m.-3 a.m. (kitchen open until 2 a.m)
Credit cards: Visa, MC, Amex, Interac
Licence: yes
Wheelchair access: not for Peel, yes for de Maisonneuve East

Peel Pub has been around for a long time and they serve good traditional tavern food at both their sites, at incredibly good prices.

The food here might not win prizes for innovation, but the selection is good and the quality is consistent. The best bets are definitely the spaghetti ($.99 any time), the excellent pig's knuckles ($5.99), and the hungry man breakfast ($3.99) which consists of two eggs, choice of meat, home fries, French toast or pancakes, toast and unlimited coffee. Breakfast is served until 11.30 a.m. daily, 4 p.m. weekends. There are three specials for each day of the week ($3.99, $4.99,.$5.99). Monday includes rib steak dinner ($5.99), Tuesday is shepherd's pie ($3.99) etc. The club sandwich ($6.99) is not only substantial, it tastes good, as do the fish and chips. Chicken wings are only 9¢ each on Sunday! Draft beer prices are certainly very low— $1.29/glass, $2.49/16-oz, $5.19/32-oz-pitcher, $9.49/60-oz-pitcher, $21.49/140-oz-pitcher.

The affable Tony Palladini manages both locations, and chefs Hector and Conroy run both kitchens. The ambiance is that of a tavern, the place is big and noisy, but the food is tasty, reliable, plentiful, and cheap, and service is friendly and efficient. Peel Pub clearly charges as little as possible for food, hoping to attract customers who will also buy the beer. It's a very old tavern tradition and it works. Peel Pub is crowded and noisy at lunch time and in the evening.

# PETER'S CAPE COD

**160 Ste-Anne**, Ste-Anne-de-Bellevue (métro Lionel-Groulx, bus 211)
457-0081
Hours: 11:30 a.m.-10 p.m. (11 p.m. in summer)
Credit cards: Visa, MC, Amex
Licence: yes
Wheelchair access: yes
Reserve on weekends and in summer

This charming Ste-Anne-de-Bellevue waterfront restaurant serves terrific fish.

This is a great spot to get away from it all—and only 30 minutes from downtown. Although they have other things, Peter's Cape Cod concentrates on fish. They have a $6.95 set menu which includes 45 items. Choices include fish and chips, clam strips, breaded shrimp, garlic shrimp, chicken brochette, spaghetti with clams, filet of doré with black bean sauce, garlic scallops, scallop brochette, Coquille St-Jacques, and some meat items such as beef brochette and chicken fingers, etc. During the summer when they are very busy and the pleasant outdoor waterfront terrace is available, this set menu remains as the lunch menu, and dinner is à la carte with higher prices. From Labour Day until mid-April the lunch menu is the basic menu, and the $6.95 includes soup and salad. Dinner is the set menu at $9.95, but without soup (except for seniors). Dessert is extra (bread pudding with lemon sauce is very good), but you may not be able to manage it—portions are generous. The à la carte menu is also available, but the $9.95 special is too appealing to pay much attention to it. The fish is always fresh and not overcooked.

The space is very warm and inviting in winter, and open and outdoorsy in summer. Service is friendly and efficient. You can have a romantic dinner here, or an evening with family and friends. At last, an affordable seafood restaurant!

# LE PETIT ALEP

**191 Jean-Talon East** (near de Gaspé, métro Jean-Talon,
92 bus)
270-9361
Hours: Monday-Friday 11 a.m.-11:30 p.m., Saturday, Sunday
9:30 a.m.-11.30 p.m.
Credit cards: Visa, MC, Amex, Interac, Diner's Club,
EnRoute
Licence: yes
Wheelchair access: yes; washrooms are through adjoining
Grand Alep.

This Middle Eastern bistro/café on Jean-Talon east is a
less expensive version of its parent, the Restaurant Alep.

The menu includes many Syrian/Armenian dishes, with
lots of cumin, coriander, cayenne, and garlic. Brunch
($7.95) is available Saturday and Sunday until 3 p.m.
Lunch specials ($7.95) include soup, salad, and a main
dish, which might be fish, or artichokes stuffed with
chicken. It's a good bet to get a selection of dishes and
share. The vegetarian plate ($10.50) includes rich and
creamy hummous, puréed eggplant, a rich orange spread
of pomegranate molasses with nuts, stuffed vine leaves,
beet salad, lentils, and rice—it goes a long way. The
sabanegh (spinach with spices in a grilled pita, with or
without cheese, $4.50, 4.75) are among an interesting
selection of appetizers which are savoury delights. The
special lamb plate ($4.75/sandwich, $9/plate )is cooked
all day with many spices and is a wonderfully rich and
delicious stew. The extraordinarily good kebab osmally
is a beef brochette slathered with tahina, garlic, nuts, and
spices ($4/sandwich, $7/plate).

The Petit Alep opened in 1995 and is run by the Frangié
sisters (Tania and Chahla) whose family owns the very
popular Restaurant Alep next door. Mother Jacqueline
cooks for both restaurants. Service is helpful and friendly
and there's a terrace in good weather. Low-key uncluttered
decorations contribute to a relaxed and inviting atmosphere.
All prices include tax. Great food! Great Prices!

# LA PETITE MARCHE

**5035 St-Denis** (near Laurier, métro Laurier, 30 bus)
842-1994
Hours: 7:45 a.m.-11 p.m.
Credit cards: none
Licence: yes
Wheelchair access: no

This small casual restaurant near the National Theatre School on St-Denis serves French and Italian bistro-style fare at rock bottom prices.

The specials of the day are an incredible deal—six choices for $6.49 including soup, dessert, and coffee! There is usually a slightly more expensive ($8.25) selection which might include seafood. The regular specials might include a trademark juicy chicken with basil or with marsala, or pasta Alfredo with mushrooms. The soups are Mediterranean style and definitely homemade. Draft micro-brewery beer is $1.95, and there are some interesting wines at good prices. The breakfast menu is available all day and includes assorted omelets for less than $4.

Mehdi Sam is the chef owner who began cooking in Morocco, and the Mediterranean influence is obvious throughout. The restaurant opened in 1994 and renovations will soon expand the available space. The kitchen is flexible and accommodating and the service is extremely friendly. There are rotating art shows on the walls, and a stand-up bar. The chairs are comfortable. The atmosphere is very casual. This place is suitable for dining alone or with friends, and kids are welcome. This is a wonderful small neighbourhood restaurant with quality homestyle cooking.

# PHILIPPINE VILLAGE

4699 Van Horne (near Victoria, métro Plamondon, bus)
731-0797
Hours: Tuesday-Thursday and Sunday 11 a.m.-midnight,
Friday-Saturday 11 a.m.- 3 a.m., closed Monday
Credit cards: Visa, MC, Amex, Interac
Licence: beer and wine
Wheelchair access: no

This Philippine restaurant in the Snowdon area serves
generous portions of wonderful food and around 8 p.m.
you get video karaoke too!

There are no daily specials here but the menu includes
a wide assortment of inexpensive dishes, and portions are
very generous. The food is mild, but good hot sauce is
available. Oxtail stewed in peanut sauce with coconut milk
and beans ($8.95) is succulent. Noodle dishes ($5.75-
$7.95) are a meal in a bowl. House specialties are chicken
in coconut cream (Ginataang Manok $8.95), and chicken
in tamarind sauce (Sinampalukang Manok $7.95), both
in rich sauce and served over rice. There are pork and
beef dishes, and an extensive seafood menu, including
shrimp, squid, and kingfish. ($4.95-$9.95).

The restaurant is a family affair—the extended Narciso
family, who have been here for about15 years, and have
worked in other restaurants before opening Philippine
Village in 1996. TV Manila is available live via satellite,
and the décor relies on ceiling fans, plastic flowers, and
palm trees. The large round tables have tablecloths under
glass, and in summer the doors in front open out to make
a semi-terrace. Staff are very helpful and will help the
uninitiated choose. Take-out and delivery (over $20) is
available. This is a good and informal eating place with
homestyle Philippine cooking, down-home atmosphere
and, if you wish, karaoke.

## PHO BAC

**1016 St-Laurent** (near la Gauchetière, métro Place d'Armes, 55 bus)
5473 Victoria (métro Côte-Ste-Catherine, 24 bus)
393-8116; 341-1265
10 a.m.-10 p.m.
Credit cards: none
Licence: beer
Wheelchair access: no

This restaurant offers simple but good Vietnamese specialties at super prices.

The specialties of the house are the wonderfully fresh and generous soup and a series of six combinations or set meals. The Chicken Tonkinoise soup ($4.35, $4.95, $5.95) is the most popular dish on the extensive menu. It is light but satisfying, redolent with fresh coriander. The combo meals are excellent value and the food is varied and good— soup, curry chicken and rice or noodles ($6.95), soup, ginger chicken ($6.95), soup and shrimp with vegetables ($7.50), and vegetarian soup, fried tofu with vegetables ($6.95). The sautéed chicken with soup ($6.95) is especially good. All the combo meals are satisfying and tasty, so order whatever strikes your fancy.

The food may not be exciting but it is good and plentiful, and offers excellent value. The décor is non-existent but the space is clean and spacious. Service is efficient but unobtrusive. They are busy but not frantic, and it is clear that people come here to eat rather than linger. The Victoria location is smaller and has a more limited menu. They opened on St-Laurent in 1995. Kids and families are very welcome here and the meals are definitely heart warming and good. This is bargain rate Vietnamese comfort food at its best.

# PHO HOA

**6208 Côte-des-Neiges** (near Van Horne, métro Côte-des-Neiges, 161, 165 bus)
343-5018
Hours: 9 a.m.-10 p.m.
Credit cards: Visa, Interac
Licence: no
Wheelchair access: no

The Pho Hoa is the only Montreal branch of a chain of Vietnamese soup restaurants that serve fresh, wholesome soups which are meals in a bowl at rock bottom prices.

There are 23 varieties of Tonkinoise soup, ranging in price from $3.75-$5.25. Choices include beef, chicken, seafood, and vegetarian, and they are all meals in themselves. All soups are served with fresh lime and fresh basil, bean sprouts, and jasmine tea. The spring rolls are fresh and crammed with shrimp and fresh mint. The seafood soup contains generous quantities of shrimp, squid, imitation crab, scallops, and noodles, as well as a beautifully flavoured broth. The meat soup ($4.25) contains eye-of-round steak, and tender flank steak, noodles and the wonderful broth. There are a few other dishes available, but the house specialty is definitely the soup.

Pho Hoa is part of a chain with 50 locations in Canada and the U.S.—but it couldn't be more unlike a fast food chain. The Montreal branch opened in 1990. The restaurant is utilitarian, and bright, efficient, and clean. There are rows of plastic topped tables and stacks of spoons, chopsticks, napkins, and hot sauce. People go to eat rather than linger, although it is comfortable and cheerful. Children, families, and large groups are all welcome here, but you can also feel comfortable eating alone. You get generous amounts of fresh, wholesome, simple food, and no frills at very low cost.

# PICK'S

**5155 de Maisonneuve West**  (Vendôme, métro Vendôme)
486-1857
Hours: noon-10 p.m., closed Sunday; in summer open until
11 p.m., except Sunday noon-8 p.m.
Credit cards: none
Licence: no
Wheelchair access: no

This Caribbean restaurant offers homestyle food which is wholesome and generous, in a small, friendly restaurant or for popular take-out or delivery, just opposite the Vendôme métro.

All meals at Pick's are served with well-prepared traditional rice and peas, and salad. Choices are available in small and large servings. The menu contains many typical dishes such as the very popular oxtail stew ($8, $11) and goat curry ($8, $11), both of which have rich and flavourful gravies. There are a number of good homemade soups ($4) available. They also have good roti: boneless chicken ($4), beef ($5), and goat ($5). Assorted Caribbean hot sauces are available. Once in a while, on the weekend, they make an excellent ackee and salt fish ($8, $11), and sometimes they prepare red snapper ($11). Call ahead to see if they have it.

Owner Winston Richard is from Jamaica but has been here for many years. He originally had a home catering business but opened Pick's in January 1996. There are lots of regulars and some people seem to eat here almost every day. The take-out and delivery is very popular, even more so because the restaurant is close to the métro and bus stop. They deliver in the neighbourhood for an $8 minimum order; further afield the minimum is $16. They cater special events if you set it up ahead. Pick's has very good West Indian fare at reasonable prices.

# LE PIN RESTAURANT

**5219 Décarie** (near Queen Mary, métro Snowdon)
485-5217
Hours: Monday, Tuesday noon-10 p.m., closed
Wednesday, Thursday- Saturday noon-10 p.m., Sunday
4 p.m.- 10 p.m.
Credit cards: Interac
Licence: no
Wheelchair access: one stair at the entrance

This small restaurant serves a very small selection of traditional homestyle Korean dishes.

The menu includes seven main course selections and the price range is $5.99-$12.99, including tax. Delicious homemade kimchi is served on the side with all orders. The house specialty is a very good cold noodle soup ($9.99), which is served with vegetables in a huge stainless steel bowl. It tastes a little like Japanese sunomono and is refreshing and filling. The dumplings ($7.99) are a generous order of homemade fresh daily dumplings with a wonderful stuffing. They can also be ordered in soup ($8.99). The sausage ($12.99) is really superb, homemade with pork, rice and black pepper. It is also available in sausage soup ($8.99). There is also a mung bean omelet ($5.99). All the food is extremely fresh and good tasting and made with healthy ingredients.

The Park family opened this restaurant in August 1997. Ki has been here for 20 years and Joung for not quite two years; young son Doyoung also helps. The space is very simple, uncluttered, and pleasant. Everything is spotlessly clean, with glass-covered white tablecloths. The Korean name of the restaurant is Choung Song Mun OK, or Pine Tree, and there is an emphasis on fresh and wholesome ingredients. The clientèle is almost exclusively Korean. This is authentic homestyle Korean food at excellent prices.

# PIZZA MOTTA

**315 Mozart East** (near Henri-Julien, métro Jean-Talon)
270-5952
Hours: 9 a.m.-9 p.m.
Credit cards: MC, Interac
Licence: no
Wheelchair access: no

Pizza Motta is the resto arm of a bakery and everything is very freshly made and served without fuss and fanfare in a family setting.

Pizzas here are wonderfully fresh and there is a wide variety of fresh vegetable topping combinations which change daily. Pizza and a salad is $4.95. The cannelloni is tasty, generous, and topped with a good sauce. The prices range between $5 and $8 and change according to what is fresh and available at the nearby Jean-Talon Market. Chicken pie and veal parmesan appear regularly. You might find stuffed peppers or eggplants, and a variety of pastas with homemade sauce. Brio is the perfect accompaniment. Hot olive and pepper antipasto is complimentary. Most things are available for take-out from the bakery, along with many Italian baked goods.

This is a family business—the bakery that grew! Many locals eat here regularly, and you can eat outside in good weather. Many people buy take-out directly from the bakery.

There is no delivery. Everything is very informal, and there are only 11 tables. The décor is far from luxurious and definitely not trendy, but the food is good and the prices are right. Families and kids are welcome.

# LOS PLANES

**531 Bélanger Eas**t (near St-Hubert, métro Jean-Talon, 95, 30 bus)
277-3675
Hours: 11 a.m.-10 p.m., closed Monday (They often stay open later on weekends.)
Credit cards: none
Licence: no
Wheelchair access: no

This delightful restaurant near Jean-Talon Market features Salvadoran specialties.

Each table has huge glass containers of homemade pickled onions, coleslaw, jalapeños, and a plain fresh tomato sauce, to which diners help themselves. There is a lunch special ($5.45) which includes generous quantities of soup, rice, salad, main dish, tortillas, dessert, and coffee. This is an amazing deal! There are some main dishes (chicken or beef burrito $7.95, rice with seafood $10.25), and they are generous enough for two, but most people order a variety of little tasties and turn them into a meal. The house specialties are pupusas, cornmeal dumplings stuffed with a variety of delicious fillings—savoury little packages ($1.35) stuffed with cheese, grilled pork, or a mixture. The tamales are made from corn flour with chicken filling, steamed in a banana leaf ($1.50)—very well prepared and delicious. Fried plantains ($2) are perfectly cooked and not greasy—apparently they are eaten in the morning in El Salvador, served sometimes with sour cream or beans ($2.95). Vegetarians can eat well here.

Gladys Beltran, along with Milago, Maria, José, and Giovanni Alexandre run the restaurant as a family enterprise. The parents have been here about 10 years and the sons arrived just a short while ago. The restaurant opened in June 1996. The atmosphere is warm and hospitable, and diners feel right at home. They are very helpful and will advise on what to order if you want help. Family-run homestyle restaurants don't get any better than this!

# PUSHAP

**5195 Paré Avenue** (near Mountain Sights, métro Namur)
737-4527
(There is another branch on the West Island, 11,999 Sources
Road, where credit cards are accepted and wine and British
beer is on tap. 683-0556)
Hours: 9 a.m.-9 p.m.
Credit cards: no
Licence: no
Wheelchair access: entrance OK, but not washroom

Pushap is a busy restaurant which serves top quality
vegetarian Indian food.

The menu includes a wide variety of homestyle Indian
vegetarian dishes. The thali special of the day ($4.95)
offers two choices of curry. Pakoras and samosas with
tamarind sauce are $1.50 for two. Vegetable dishes include
potatoes and cauliflower ($3), eggplant ($2.50), okra
($3.50), and zucchini ($3). Special dishes include a wonderful potato and yam curry ($2.50), and an outstanding
eggplant/tomato curry. Chapati is $0.50 and pratha is
$1.50. Sweets are homemade and there are always at least
a dozen choices ($1.25 a piece) including milk cake, ladoo,
barfi, and the best of all, gajrela (carrot cake). Spices here
are handled with a deft and knowing hand, and ingredients
are always fresh. Pushap doesn't take shortcuts, and it
shows.

Sister/brother Mila and Jit look after the front and other
members of this extended family produce the great North-
ern Indian vegetarian cuisine. Their mother handles the
kitchen at Paré Street. The service is always friendly, and
regulars are greeted by name. Things sometimes get
harried, but who cares, the food is worth it. The Paré branch
has only 20 seats and there are often lineups for take-out,
which is a large part of their business. People come from
all over the city for the sweets, which are available for
take-out by the pound. Pushap is a winner on all scores!

# RELAIS DES SULTANS

**!0 Notre-Dame West** (near Guy, métro Lucien Lallier, 35 bus)
934-4655
Hours: 11 a.m.-10 p.m., closed Sunday
Credit cards: Visa, MC, Amex, Interac
Licence: yes
Wheelchair access: no

This small charming restaurant on Notre-Dame near Guy has spectacularly good Mediterranean food.

The chef-owner establishes a monthly table d'hôte menu which contains good variety, and includes appetizer, homemade dessert and beverage. A typical menu might include several couscous selections ($9-$12.50), several tagines (Moroccan stew, $10-$13.50), three or four different pastas ($9.50), eggplant parmesan ($9.50) and chicken brochette. Each month is different. Pasta and baklava are made fresh daily on the premises, the tagines are heavenly combinations, and the couscous is bursting with freshness and flavour. The à la carte menu contains many couscous possibilities, from the straightforward vegetarian ($7.50) to the sumptuous seafood ($22.95). Hummous ($3.50), brik ($5.95), and Middle Eastern pizzas ($6.50-$8.95) are also available. The lunch menu ($8.50) includes salad, main course, beverage, and baklava.

Owner-chef Omar Alyafie is a treasure—he really knows how to cook! He is from Yemen but worked for a number of years as a couscous and grill specialist at Club Med. He learned to cook Italian from his southern Italian former partner. When the restaurant first started, his mother baked the baklava every day, but since her return to Yemen Omar bakes it himself. Occasionally a typical Yemenite dish is included on the menu. This charming restaurant seats 32, has white tablecloths, and is ideal for a special night out. This restaurant is a real winner.

# RESTAURANT SÉNÉGALAISE

**66 St-Viateur West** (near Clark, métro St-Laurent, 55 bus)
273-7001
Hours: 5 p.m.-10:30 p.m., closed Monday and Tuesday
Credit cards: none
Licence: no
Wheelchair access: entrance OK, washroom a problem

This small informal restaurant on the Plateau serves excellent Senegalese food at unbelievable prices.

There is a list of five or six daily specials posted every day, all under $6. The cooking is typical of West African home cooking and food is slow cooked to perfection. The chicken yassa ($4.99) is made with lemon and onion, the chicken maffé ($4.99) is with peanut sauce, and the thiebouiene ($5.99) is fish marinated in spices and fried. The menu sometimes includes couscous with chicken or meat. A variety of stewed dishes is usually available. The food is satisfying and savoury, with rich tasty gravies, served over rice. There is usually a vegetarian choice available.

Owner Papa Diep (formerly of Teranga) opened this restaurant in October 1996. It has only 16 seats and is informal and relaxed. Everyone is very helpful and they are genuinely interested in introducing people to Senegalese cuisine, customs, and culture. Take-out is popular and they will deliver in the neighbourhood. They do catering, offering 30 choices of African food. The space is small, basic, but clean and comfortable, and the atmosphere is friendly. The food is authentic homestyle cooking and you get very good value.

# RESTAURANT STEVE-ANNA

**3290 Bélanger East** (near St-Michel, métro St-Michel, 67 or 95 bus)
725-3776
Hours: Monday-Saturday 9 a.m.-9 p.m., closed Sunday
Credit cards: none
Licence: BYOB
Wheelchair access: entry OK, washroom could be a problem

This Haitian restaurant in the north end is small but serves excellent homestyle Haitian specialties, and the prices are really affordable.

Specials change daily and include rice, plantains/sweet potato, coleslaw and a main dish, and the price range is $7-$10. The food is flavourful and not very spicy. Many of the specials are long, slowly simmered stews. Choices usually include fried chicken, beef, and vegetable stew, fried fish, and they sometimes have lambi, a beautifully prepared conch stew. Rice and beans are always available. Ask for Anna's homemade sauce; it's outstanding! The food is homestyle and good.

There are not many tables. Everyone lines up near the door and you choose what you want at the counter. Everything is placed in a take-out container, even if you are eating there, and portions are large. The restaurant is near a grocery store of the same name which Steve Jacrois started in 1985. His sister, Anna Domond, had a take-out counter in the back of the store, but she moved it here in 1993. This operation is evolving nicely. There are lots of regulars and much of the business is take-out, although you can eat there as well. Good stuff!

# ROSIE'S

**3655 St-Laurent** (near Pine, métro St-Laurent, 55 bus)
no telephone
Hours: Saturday-Wednesday 11:30 a.m.-7 p.m., Thursday,
Friday 11:30 a.m.-10 p.m.
Credit cards: none
Licence: no
Wheelchair access: no

Rosie's is a funky snack bar with character on the Main
where you can find good food and good company.

The menu includes lunch specials (add 50¢ in the
evening): burger (choice of meat, veggie, or fish), potatoes
and beverage) for $3.95, soup and grilled cheese sandwich
with beverage for $3, or large soup with salad and beverage
for $3.50. Fresh juices are $1.50/$2.50, and homemade
soups are satisfying. There is a limited selection of à la
carte items: veggie burger ($3.75), Rosie burger ($4.25
with bacon, sautéed onions and mushrooms), Tex-mex
burger ($4.75 with salsa, sour cream, chili, grated cheese,
and avocado), fishburger ($2.75) and vegetarian chili
($2.50). The burgers are unfailingly moist and fresh, and
are served on a fresh crusty Vienna roll. Fish and chips
($4.25) are excellent. Vegetarians do well here. Delicious
desserts (pecan pie, banana cake, and apple betty) are
homemade.

Rosie's is at the back of the ground floor of a vintage
building on the Main. It's a well-kept secret for the regulars
who enjoy Shyam Amsel's good food and good company.
He is a big gentle man who brings good humour to this
tiny unlikely snack bar with seven stainless steel tables.
He has cooked in ashrams in India, Woodstock, N.Y. and
Oregon, and at Bimbo's on Fairmount. Rosie's is a good
place to go when you are shopping on the Main, before
going to a movie, or when you want to enjoy simple but
tasty food .

# ROTISSERIE PORTUGALIA

**34 Rachel West** (near St-Laurent, métro St-Laurent, 55 bus)
282-1519
Hours: 10 a.m.-10 p.m.
Credit cards: no
Licence: yes
Wheelchair access: no

Vegetarians should skip Rôtisserie Portugalia altogether—
this restaurant features authentic Portuguese grilled meat
at its finest!

The menu is short and simple but offers tempting
examples of just how succulent grilled meat can be. A
whole churrasco chicken—flattened, and marinated in
spicy house sauce, then grilled slowly—is $9.50 if you
take it out, and $15 if you have it in the restaurant with
fries (frozen) and salad. Half a chicken in the restaurant is
$8. You will have to share! Other specialties include cod
($9), sardines ($6), ribs ($6.50) steak, and pork ($6). Fiery
piri-piri sauce is featured in the marinades. A carnivore's
heaven, the grilled meat is the star!

Owner Alnico Costa is Portuguese, but he has lived in
Angola, so this style of cooking could legitimately be
called Afro-Lusitanian. This restaurant still caters to a
largely Portuguese clientèle, but they are invariably warm
and friendly. The exterior looks like a neighbourhood
greasy spoon. Rôtisserie Portugalia is a tiny hole-in-the-
wall, with a small unpretentious dining room where you
find blue gingham tablecloths and pictures of local soccer
teams. As you step inside, the small space is dominated
by a large charcoal grill with a few stools at the counter.
The aromas of grilling marinated meat are overwhelming
and wonderful. They do a booming take-out business.
Since everything is grilled to order, call at least a half
hour ahead to order the chicken for take-out. Once you
try this you'll never again be content with a standard BBQ
chicken!

# SABOUYOUMA

**4539 St-Laurent** (near Mont-Royal, métro Mont-Royal, 55 bus)
288-8063
Hours: 5 p.m.-11 p.m., closed Monday (may be open at noon during the summer)
Credit cards: Visa, Interac
Licence: yes
Wheelchair access: no

This small restaurant on the Plateau serves wonderful Senegalese and Ivory Coast food.

There are daily specials but only at lunch. The menu is somewhat limited for now and is à la carte. Choices include a variety of main courses including the superb yassa, lemon-marinated chicken ($6.99) served over rice with a rich and plentiful lemony sauce, okra ($6.99), tasty mafé, chicken with peanut sauce ($6.99), and a wonderful braised fish with boiled plantain ($10.99). Vegetarian dishes are available on request. Fried plantain with salad ($3.99) and avocado with shrimp ($ 4.75) are also available. Tropical fruit juices ($1.75) and ginger juice ($2) are available

The restaurant opened in the summer of 1997 and it is evolving. Chef Odette comes from Ivory Coast. Staff are warm and welcoming. They are eager to share their cuisine and culture and are very helpful. The ambiance is good and the decor is attractive. Kids are certainly welcome. There is live West African music from time to time on weekends, and you can call to check. They do take-out. The cooking is authentic West African, homestyle, and the chef has a nice touch.

# ST-VIATEUR BAGEL & CAFÉ

**1127 Mont-Royal East** (near Christophe-Colomb, métro Mont-Royal, 97 bus)
528-6361
Hours: 6 a.m.-midnight
Credit cards: none
Licence: wine & beer served; liquor is only served in coffee
Wheelchair access: one step at entrance

The St-Viateur Bagel is now available on Mont-Royal East—and it's all dressed!

These are genuine Montreal bagels to be eaten here or for take-out—plain or pressed (grilled). The bagel spreads include the classic cream cheese ($1.95) and even hummous ($2.95). Salads ($6-$7.95) are available but the most popular items are bagel sandwiches with soup or a salad (the artichoke salad is huge and delicious). Selections include coque/egg and tomato ($3.95), coque deluxe/cooked egg and ham ($4.95), veggie deluxe/provolone, asparagus, hearts of palm, broccoli, tomato ($6.95), à la grècque/feta, tomato, cucumber, olive oil, and olives ($6.95). The most popular are the traditional ($7.95) smoked salmon with cream cheese, and the pressed roast beef ($5.95) with Swiss cheese, olive oil, and tomato. The bagels are tender, slightly smoky, chewy, and tasty—just as you would expect them to be. Fillings are very generous, all ingredients are top quality, Italian coffee is excellent, and desserts are delicious if you have room..

Vince Morena started rolling bagels at age 13! He made a family deal with dad Joe Morena to license the St-Viateur Bagel name and recipe. He took two bagel makers with him, designed a modern café where centre-stage is the huge wood-burning brick bagel oven in which some of the world's best bagels are baked, and the café opened in 1996. It works. People are gobbling up the truly delectable bagel sandwiches, lingering over coffee, talking, or reading selections from the magazine rack. Of course you can leave with a bagful of bagels. GREAT BAGELS, GREAT IDEA!

# SANS MENU

**3714 Notre-Dame West** (near Bourget, métro Lionel Groulx)
933-4782
Hours: Monday & Tuesday 11:30 a.m.-9 p.m., Wednesday-
Friday 11:30-10 p.m., Saturday 5 p.m.-10 p.m.,
closed Sunday
Licence: yes
Credit cards: none
Wheelchair access: a two-inch step at front door
Reservations preferable

This jewel of a resto in the middle of working class St-
Henri is an unlikely spot for fine French cuisine!

The blackboard menu features nine or ten selections
for the daily special, ($9.65-$14.95 including tax). Each
meal includes a choice of appetizer (typically a homemade
terrine, special salad, or mousseline), a main course, and
coffee or tea. Main course selections might include a
chicken dish such as poulet citron (delicately lemon-
flavoured breast of chicken served with exquisite French-
style home fries), house specialty salade farfelue (strips
of smoked salmon, feta cheese, and prosciutto over
vegetables and greens), perhaps an exquisite lapin à la
moutarde (rabbit cooked to perfection), and a dish with
salmon cooked just right and served with seasonal
vegetables. Desserts include crème caramel and a truly
fabulous sugar pie. Micro-brewery beers and a good
selection of wine at reasonable prices are available. Lunch
specials begin at $7.50

Despite the neon signs of a pharmacy across the street,
a charming atmosphere prevails. Colette Marchessault and
partner Pierre Baudin opened the restaurant in 1992. Pierre
is the chef and Colette handles the floor. The service is
fast and efficient. The food is fabulous and offers
tremendous value. The décor is uncluttered and elegant.
This is a great choice for a special romantic evening out.
You'll never feel you are on a budget. At Sans Menu you
get quality French cuisine at unheard of prices—without
the snobbery!

# WARTZ'S
## (MONTREAL HEBREW DELICATESSEN)

3895 St-Laurent Blvd. (near Duluth, St-Laurent métro, 55 bus)
842-4813
Hours: Monday-Thursday 9 a.m.-1 a.m., Friday 9 a.m.-2 p.m., Saturday 9 a.m.- 3 a.m., Sunday 9 a.m.-1 p.m.
Credit cards: no
Licence: no
Wheelchair access: no

Schwartz's on the Main is Montreal smoked meat at its very best—perhaps even Montreal at its best.

Schwartz's smoked meat is justly legendary. The smoked brisket is juicy, tender, perfectly spiced, and it tastes divine! The most popular meal choice is the sandwich ($3.50), fries ($1.20), a dill pickle ($1), and a black cherry soda ($1.10). The sandwiches are made of piping hot smoked meat piled high on fresh sourdough rye bread. The fries are freshly made (not frozen), and are perfectly fried in vegetable oil. Pickles are Mrs. Whyte's. Smoked meat plates ($7.50/$9) are also popular. A terrific steak grilled over charcoal, with all the trimmings, is recommended if you are feeling particularly ravenous ($11.95 including small side order of liver and frankfurter). Take-out (sandwiches and cold meat by the pound) is big here—you can also buy excellent smoked chicken and ducks, and order smoked turkeys during holiday seasons.

The restaurant has an old-time deli atmosphere all its own, and barely enough room to move. Expect long lineups on weekends, but it is always worth the wait. Most waiters have been there for many years, and the service is quick and efficient. Schwartz's distinctive Rumanian-style smoked meat has become known as Montreal smoked meat and it is the standard against which all others are measured, at least in this city. It is often brought, on request, to far flung parts of the world, to provide expatriates and one-time visitors with a Schwartz's fix. IT DOESN'T GET ANY BETTER THAN THIS!

# SOUVENIRS DE BANGKOK

**1925 Ste-Catherine West** (near Fort, métro Guy-Concordia)
938-2235
Hours: 11 a.m.-3 p.m., 5 p.m.-10 p.m., closed for lunch on
weekends
Credit cards: Visa, MC, Amex, Interac
Licence: BYOB
Wheelchair access: one step at entrance

This popular Thai restaurant downtown serves good food
at very reasonable prices.

The lunch specials are extensive and complete meals
are $4.95-$8.95. There is a special menu (including soup,
imperial roll, beverage, or dessert) available between 5
and 7 p.m., including delicious pad Thai ($7.50), chicken
with crispy spinach ($8.25, lemon grass grilled chicken
or beef ($8.95), or meal combos for two for $16.95. The
regular menu is very extensive (114 items) and includes
almost anything you may want to order. The portions are
very large and the meal specials include enough food for
both you and a doggie bag. The food is very well prepared,
tasty, and well presented. The pad Thai is authentic as are
other dishes.

The Sam family opened this restaurant in 1995, and with
friends, run it as a family business. The décor is discreet,
the chairs are comfortable, and the atmosphere is pleasant.
Early in the evening there are many families, and kids are
welcome. This restaurant is also suitable for a special night
out. Reservations are recommended; they can get very
busy. The kitchen is very well organized though, and
things usually seem to run smoothly. Souvenirs de
Bangkok is extremely popular and justifiably so—the food
is good, the space is attractive, and the prices are very
reasonable, especially for downtown!

# SUN SHING

**5255 Queen Mary Road** (near Décarie, métro Snowdon, 17, 51, 166 bus)
484-3046
Hours: Sunday-Thursday 11 a.m.-11 p.m., Friday-Saturday 11 a.m.-11:30 p.m.
Credit cards: Visa, MC
Licence: yes
Wheelchair access: yes

It's a long-standing tradition to have good Chinese food at Queen Mary and Décarie, and Sun Shing picks up the mantle!

The menu here is largely Cantonese, with some Szechuan dishes. The famous Combo specials include everything and are $4.25+ at lunch and $4.50-$7.95 for dinner. The pineapple chicken is especially wonderful, not at all the overly sweet breaded goo that is often served, but real diced, unbreaded chicken breast in a delicate pineapple sauce ($5.25 including spring roll, chicken with cashews, and chicken fried rice)—amazing! Chicken dishes are particularly good, and portions are huge. The spring rolls are delicately flavoured and delicious. Vegetarian choices are interesting. Combos even include tea and fortune or almond cookies. Single dish meals are also available at very good prices, and are great value. The soups are worth trying.

Sun Shin is owned by Kenny Yang and it has been open since 1995. It occupies the space of the venerable but long-gone House of Wong which served Chinese food in this space for decades. It is an honorable replacement and a justly popular spot. The food is far superior to any of the traditional Chinese buffets and the price is right.

# TASCA

**172 Duluth East** (near Hôtel-de-Ville, métro Sherbr~~oo~~
or 55 bus)
987-1530
Hours: Monday-Wednesday 5 p.m.-11 p.m., Thursday-
Saturday noon-11 p.m.
Credit cards: Visa, MC, Amex
Licence: yes
Wheelchair access: no

This Portuguese eatery on the Plateau has a wonderful
grill menu.

Tasca has two different menus: a more expensive table
d'hôte and an à la carte menu with a wide variety of
excellent Portuguese specialties, and a limited but
marvellous bistro menu of charcoal grill items, all under
$8. Ask for it specifically if it is not on the table. The
bistro menu includes a half chicken ($6.95), pork steak
($7.95), quail ($7.95), and spareribs ($7.95). The chicken,
pork and quail are particularly recommended. Portions
are generous and accompanying salad and homemade fries
are very good. Delicious crusty Portuguese buns, and
complimentary olives and mussels round out the meal.
The charcoal grill is expertly staffed and the food is cooked
to perfection. This is not gourmet food with long
preparation and complex tastes (for that, go to the more
expensive menu), but excellent grilled food at its best.
Wines are not expensive here, and they also serve port.

Tasca is pleasant and relaxing. There are tablecloths in
the large room and great Portuguese music plays in the
background. Florindo Fazendeiro recently bought Tasca
and he has reorganized the space somewhat but the food
is just as good. Kids are comfortable here. Service can be
slow if the grill has to be started up. Tasca is suitable for
a family dinner or a special evening.

# TEHRAN

**5065 de Maisonneuve West** (métro Vendôme)
488-0400
Hours: noon-11 p.m., closed Monday
Credit cards: no
Licence: no
Wheelchair access: no
Reservations on weekend evenings

This family-run Iranian restaurant serves up authentic Persian food in a family-style restaurant.

The menu here is small and posted on the blackboard, but the food is authentic and good. Specials ($7-$8) are available all day; they change daily, but can include fish (Tuesday) and lamb shank (Thursday). There are a limited number of regular menu items, but the beef and chicken brochettes are good bets, and the marinated salmon is extraordinary. All meals include a mixed salad with a delightful yogurt dressing. Servings are very large, and you may not be able to finish your plate! Spicing is subtle and the food is a real pleasure to eat. Sumac flakes, a traditional Iranian seasoning, is found on every table. Spiced tea is included and is a great way to end a meal. The food is excellent.

The restaurant opened in 1992 and is run by a father and son, occasionally assisted by other family members. The clientèle is about half Iranian. This is a friendly, relaxed place to eat, with Iranian music playing in the background, although it gets quite busy on weekend evenings. They also do catering and take-out.

## LE TOASTEUR

**950 Roy East** (near Mentana, métro Sherbrooke, 24 bus)
527-8500
Hours: Monday-Friday7 a.m.-10 p.m., Saturday,
Sunday 7 a.m.-6 p.m.
Credit card: Visa, Amex, Interac
Licence: yes
Wheelchair access: no

This neighbourhood resto near Parc Lafontaine serves breakfast and burgers at all hours of the day, every day.

They do breakfast well and without fanfare. Eggs are cooked perfectly, as ordered, and are well presented. The Toasteur special ($6.95) includes two eggs, two meats, baked beans, French toast, and a pancake, and is definitely for Big Hungry! The more healthful alternative ($7.25) will make you feel virtuous—two poached eggs, cheddar cheese, fresh fruit, yogurt, whole wheat bread and herbal tea. The special omelet ($7.95) is made with veggies, choice of meat, creamy béchamel sauce, and cheese (meltingly yummy!), with coffee, toast, and potatoes. They serve eggs benedict or eggs florentine ($5.75/one egg, $7.25/two eggs). Pancake combinations (banana, apple, mushroom/sausage, vegetarian, etc.), waffles, and French toast are available in half or heaping full orders ($3.25-$8.75). A few sandwiches and salads and the burger special ($4.95) are also available. Freshly squeezed juices in sizes small to jumbo ($1.50-$4) are excellent.

Owner Ghyslain Boudreau strikes a balance between traditional breakfast and more healthy and  modern alternatives. The nice touches are flowers, mirrors, and stained glass (so appropriate for this neighbourhood where it is an old tradition), and the corner location ensures good natural light. The atmosphere is amiable, and you can linger over an espresso ($1.50) or cappuccino ($2.25). Sundays at noon there can be a small lineup, but there is no problem at other times.

## TRAMONTANE

3765 **Clark** (near Bernard, 55 or 80 bus)
277-1601
Hours: Tuesday-Thursday 5 p.m.-10 p.m., Friday- Saturday
5 p.m.-midnight, closed Sunday and Monday (open at lunch
in the summer)
Credit cards: Visa
Licence: yes
Wheelchair access: no

This Plateau bistro specializes in French and Catalan
cuisine. The menu is written daily on the blackboard and
changes according to the inclinations of the chef. The
selection often includes boar, quail, lamb, chicken, rabbit,
pork, and fish. The tapas are Catalan all the way and you
can have a meal of 3 for $10.25, with 12 choices available.
The cargolades (snails in spicy sauce) is especially
memorable but all are good. The table d'hôte is usually
between $9.50 and $15, including beverage and dessert.
The food is invariably cooked beautifully, with unusual
and flavourful surprises. The wonderful quail with raisins
is typical of the table d'hôte ($9.75), sautéed de-boned
quail in a white wine/muscat raisin sauce. More expensive
choices are also available and you can place an order a
day ahead for excellent paella ($15/person) or sarsuela
($18/person).

Chef Pascal Lleres and maître d' Frédéric di Bisceglie
opened this restaurant in September 1995 and it is clearly
a labour of love for both. Pascal is French and Catalan
and learned to cook under the watchful eye of his Catalan
grandmother, with professional training later in Switzer-
land. Frédéric is from Grenoble. Unpretentious, pleasant,
and welcoming, they have infused this place with charm.
There is a sidewalk terrace in good weather. It's unusual
to find food of this quality at these prices. This is a good
bet!

# TUTTO BENE

**120 St-Viateur West** (near St-Urbain, 55 or 80 bus)
270-4557
Hours: Monday-Friday 7:30 a.m.-11 p.m., Saturday 7:30
a.m.-midnight, Sunday noon-8 p.m.
Credit cards: none
Licence: no
Wheelchair access: no

This newly-opened Italian bistro serves terrific panini and
brick oven pizzas in the heart of the Plateau.

The grilled panini are fresh and really good, with interesting combinations such as grilled eggplant with pesto,
spinach, and cheese ($3.50), and chicken with provolone
($3.75). There is a combo plate ($5.50) which includes manicotti, grilled veggies, sausage, and rosemary roasted potatoes. The pizzas are delicious and slightly smoky ($5.95-
$11.95). Create your own pita pizza, $3.40 for one topping,
$4.85 for two, $4.45 for three and 85¢ for each additional.
Topping choices include porchetta, eggplant, pesto,
pancetta, and sun-dried tomatoes. Good vegetarian choices
are available. Brio goes well with everything and good
espresso and cappuccino are available. There is also a
lunch special available. The pizza dessert ($6.95) is fun,
with amaretto, apples, and caramel.

Rocco Furfaro opened this cheerful and relaxed place
in summer 1997. There is a wood-burning pizza oven and
the pizza crusts are suitably smoky and crisp. There are
not many seats but there is space between the tables and
diners are not cramped. Take-out is especially popular.
One wall is covered with appetizing jars and bottles of
preserves: peppers, tomatoes, fruit, vinegars, sauces,
pickles. You order at the counter while Italian pop music
plays in the background. Service is friendly and efficient.
This is a good place to eat alone or in a small group. Kids
and adults alike will surely find something to please, and
it sure beats any fast food chain.

# VILLAGE MON NAN

**1098 Clark Street** (near René-Lévesque, métro St-Laurent, or 55 bus)
879-9680
Hours: Sunday-Thursday 11 a.m.-11 p.m., Friday-Saturday 11 a.m.-midnight
Credit cards: Visa, MC, Amex
Licence: yes
Wheelchair access: no

Village Mon Nan in Chinatown serves Peking and Shanghai food. .

The menu contains a whole range of Peking and Shanghai style food but it is the Peking Duck special ($21.95) which is especially attractive and which is available at all times without pre-ordering. The duck is still served in three delicious courses: sliced thin with crispy skin intact, to be rolled up into small pancakes with scallions and hoisin sauce; a duck and vegetable dish; and finally as duck soup with thin clear noodles. The duck dinner feeds three, but if you are more than three, you might really enjoy some delicious dumplings (fried or steamed) as a preliminary ($4.75/order), or some of the other tempting goodies on the full menu.

This is a very pleasant restaurant upstairs from the Mon Nan (John Lee manages both) which serves Cantonese food. Village Mon Nan is the successor to the old Shantung Restaurant which for several years was the only place in Chinatown where you could always get Peking duck. Chef Yip moved here, with all his Peking duck secrets. The Peking Duck is unequivocally the best in Chinatown. They are fortunate to have the talents of Chef Yip—and so are we!

## VILLA WELLINGTON

**4701 Wellington** (Verdun, near 2nd Avenue, de l'Église métro)
768-0102
Hours: Tuesday-Sunday 11 a.m.-11 p.m.
Credit cards: Visa, MC
Licence: yes
Wheelchair access: one small step at entrance

This Verdun neighbourhood restaurant serves an interesting variety of Peruvian food.

Potatoes are native to Peru and Peruvians are very partial to them. The menu here includes many different kinds of potatoes—all deliciously prepared. The daily soup is a good buy at $1.99/85¢ with a meal. The daily specials include an appetizer and a main dish with vegetables. Appetizer choices include a stuffed potato, tamales, and boiled potatoes with a cheese sauce. Main dishes for the specials include: marinated chicken ($7.95), beef stew with coriander ($7.50), and fried pork ($7.95). There are also many à la carte dishes such as ceviche ($10), seafood soup ($12.99), grilled fish ($8.50), delicious fried squid, and grilled trout ($8.50). The fried seafood plate for two is so wonderful it defies description. It's best to forget the desserts. There is also a choice of non-Peruvian dishes, basic Italian and Greek food, but go for the Peruvian specialties which are not as readily available elsewhere.

The decor is Peruvian, with hand woven tablecloths under plastic, and paper placemats. The atmosphere is that of a neighbourhood family restaurant. Although the staff is Latin, the clientèle is mixed. There is Latin music and a good feeling about the place. Owner Augusto Saravia is a Peruvian who now lives in Verdun—he opened the restaurant in 1992. You will enjoy the food here, especially the potatoes! Corona beer ($3.95) goes very well with the Peruvian specialties.

# THE SEX OF RESTAURANTS

by Josh Freed

There is no task more daunting to the average anglo than making a restaurant reservation—the ultimate cultural survival test.

In Ontario, any fool can make a reservation—you just open the phone book and look up your restaurant. But in Quebec, you must first know the *sex* of your restaurant.

Let's say you want a reservation at a little place you heard about from some friends—the Viaduc restaurant.

But is it masculine: le Viaduc? Or feminine: la Viaduc? Or could it be listed under something tricky—like Le Restaurant La Viaduc?

It's not easy to remember your genders when you're standing in a phone booth, in -34°, with your gloves off. And even when you consult your pocket dictionary and find that Viaduc is masculine, your search has just begun.

Is it Restaurant Le Viaduc, or Restaurant du Viaduc? Restaurant les Viaducs, or Restaurant des Viaducs? All are grammatically correct.

It could also be listed under Restaurant Chez Viaduc or Restaurant Chez le Viaduc (over 100 restaurants are listed under Chez alone). Not to mention Restaurant au Viaduc, Restaurant aux Viaducs or Le Restaurant aux Viaducs.

Get one pronoun wrong and you eat at home.

And who's to say the Viaduc is actually classified as a restaurant? It might be listed as a café, and if so, is it a café-restaurant or a restaurant-café?

Or could it be something trendy, like a café-terrace? Each of these have separate listings—hundreds of pages apart.

You don't believe me? Check the Montreal phone book. There are listings for Restaurant-bars and Bar- restaurants.

For Restaurant-bistros and Bistro-cafés. There are Restaurant-charcuteries, Restaurant-patisseries, Restaurant-pizzerias and Restaurant-brochetteries.

Not to mention Brochetterie-restaurants.

It's not easy being an anglophone on the telephone. Or afterwards. Because once you've found your restaurant and showed up for your reservation, you still have to order.

Hmmm—now what's the sex of Caesar salad?

From *Fear of Frying and Other Fax of Life* by Josh Freed. Winner of the 1995 Stephen Leacock Prize for Humour. Published by Véhicule Press.

# Indexes

## SPECIALTY INDEX

**French**
Bistro Unique 31
Sans Menu 93

**Haitian**
Restaurant Steve-Anna 88

**Indian**
Apna Tandoor 24
Pushap 85

**Iranian**
Byblos 33
Copoli 46
Tehran 98

**Italian**
Agostini 21
Amelio's 22
Café International 35
Café Presto 36
Capoli 46
Elio Pizzeria 50
Manzo Pizza 63
Motta 83
Relais des Sultans 86
Tutto Bene 101

**Kid Friendly**
Briskets 32
Chalet Bar B-Q 40
Elio Pizzeria 50
Motta 83
Galaxie Diner 54
Manzo Pizza 63
Ma-am-m Bolduc!
Mr. Steer 70
Tutto Bene 61
Village Mon Nan 102

**Korean**
Pin (Le) 82

**Kosher**
Ernie & Ellie's 52

**Lebanese**
Farrouj 53

**Mexican**
Iza 58

**Middle Eastern**
Farrouj 53
Petite Alep (Le) 76

**Morroccan**
Bedouin's House 26

**North African**
Bedouin's House 26
Mediterranéan, La 66
Relais des Sultan 86
  (Bistro le)

**Peruvian**
Villa Wellington 103

**Philippino**
Philippine Village 78

**Polish**
Mazurka 64

**Portuguese**
Bistro Le Porto 30
Chez Doval 42
Rotisserie Portugalia 90

**Pub**
McKibbins 65
Peel Pub 74

**Québécois**
Binerie Mont-Royal (Le) 28
Ma-am-m Bolduc! 62

**Russian**
Metropole (La) 68

**Salvadoran**
Caretta (La) 39
Planes (Los) 84

**Seafood**
Moules & Cie 69
Peter's Cape Cod 75

**Senegalese**
Restaurant Sénégalaise 87
Sabouyouma 91

**Sports Bar**
Café International 35
Champs 41

**Sri Lanken**
Genuine Restaurant 55

**Syrian/Armenian**
Petit Alep (Le) 76

**Thai**
Bangkok 25
Pattaya 73
Souvenirs de Bangkok 95

**Tibetan**
Chez Gatsé 43

**Tunisian**
Mediterranéan (La) 66

**Vegetarian**
Café Santropol 37
Chez Soi 44
Pushap 85

**West Indian**
Caribbean Curry House 38
Jardin du Cari 59
Pick's 81

**Vietnamese**
Chez Tung 45
Cristal de Saigon 48
Dong Que 49
Harmonie d'Asie (L') 57
Pho Bac 79
Pho Hoa 80

# GEOGRAPHICAL INDEX

## THE EDITORS

Nancy Marrelli and Simon Dardick are the publishers of Véhicule Press. Simon runs the day-to-day operations of the Press. Nancy is also the Director of Archives at Concordia University, Montreal.

They love to eat out.

# SEND US YOUR SUGGESTIONS

We would love to receive your suggestions for
future editions of *Cheap Thrills*. Send us the
name, address, and telephone number of the
restaurant and include a short description.

vpress@cam.org

Véhicule Press
P.O.B. 125, Place du Parc Station
Montreal, Quebec  H2W 2M9

**Visit us on the Web**
http://www.cam.org/~vpress

Véhicule Press